POTUS 2024
Balance the Scale

Booker Garvey III

Published by:

LOTT Leaders of Tomorrow, Today
PO Box 39
Nazareth, MI 49074

First Edition

POTUS 2024: Balance the Scale

Copyright © 2025

LOTT Leaders of Tomorrow, Today
All rights reserved.

ISBN: 978-1-7356687-5-8

Graphic Designer: LOTT Art Department

Editor: LOTT Writing Department

Declaration

This book is dedicated to the United States of America. The world has truly changed in the thirty-seven years I've been alive. I was too young to remember anything outside of homelife, Anita Baker, and Muhammad Ali in the 1980s.

But the 1990s… the '90s were the golden years for movies, acting, music, song writing, storytelling, and vocal composition. I'm standing on a soapbox.

This is a dedication. I dedicate this book to ALL Americans. Read this next sentence carefully. Everything isn't funny or for social media. Be serious about SOMETHING! Put a team together and make a play! The world is waiting on your impact.

If you're a parent, make sure you're serious about RAISING those babies. Every blank canvas has the potential to be a masterpiece. Paint each brush stroke with love and happiness. A little each day paints the best portrait you're capable of creating. Then admire your work.

"Make a Splash in the World"

www.LOTT48203.com

Disclaimer:

POTUS 2024: Balance The Scale is based on a true story. Some events have been dramatized, combined, or shifted chronologically for timing purposes. However, a lot of the story's contents happened in real life.

POTUS 2024: Balance The Scale was inspired by documenting and participating in the candidacy for President of the United States by the author of the book.

This work of literature is for adult audiences and is not suitable for children. It contains graphic language, adult situations, and mature sexual content.

ARTICLES:

Declaration

Preamble

I.	Black Ice	Pg 3
II.	What's a Debit Card?	Pg 10
III.	Follow Me!	Pg 22
IV.	Balance the Scale	Pg 26
V.	Campaign Announcement	Pg 30
VI.	On the Road	Pg 36
VII.	Get Back to Work	Pg 43
VIII.	My Type of Lady	Pg 47
IX.	World War Willis	Pg 52
X.	Sabbatical	Pg 61
XI.	Third Party	Pg 93
XII.	Speech!	Pg 108
XIII.	Headed West	Pg 127
XIV.	Homecoming	Pg 153

POTUS 2028 Preview

Preamble

"I'm running for president." Booker was fearless with his words. The confidence in his tone made it seem as though he'd given the idea some serious thought.

"My head hurts," Garvey replied.

His disbelief brought emotions about his body that he never felt before. Booker Garvey II had heard many things come from his son's mouth. But the latest was so unfathomable, it caused pain just behind his temple.

Holding his head in his hands, only Garvey knew the thoughts racing through his mind. Trying his best to find the words to say, he chose not to speak while his boy turned man continued.

"I'm serious." He laughed. "I'm thirty-six now. Why not? Trump and Biden did it."

"That's because of Obama."

"Maybe, but they still did it. If I don't do it now, I'll have to wait four more years. What's the worst that could happen, I win?"

"Trip, stop. Please, stop and I'm not even playing."

"Dad, look. Hear me out. I got these books for sale, right? I can use the publicity from running for president to sell books. It's perfect. This is a publicity stunt."

Garvey looked at his son wondering where he went wrong for him to be living in such a pipedream at his age. Digging deep into the thoughts of his mind, he was back at it attempting to choose his words carefully. Just in case his son was able to pull off a miracle.

"You'd need signatures, a vice president, registration forms, signs, bookings, a Campaign Manager—"

"Yeah, if I was trying to win. This is a publicity stunt!" Booker repeated. "I don't care if I get three votes, as long as I sell a million plus books." Booker shrugged. "Winning is a loss in my eyes. If I win, I'll reject it... I think."

"Three votes?" Holding his forehead, Garvey continued to wonder.

"Me, you, and Mom *at least* I'd hope. Dad, this is a publicity stunt!" Booker shouted again. "Matter of fact if I win, I will accept. Then change the world. It can't be that hard. I can do it in four years with all those resources for sure."

2024 minus 1987 equals thirty-six and some change. He is over thirty-five... He's a teacher without political experience. Is this guy high? "Are you high?" Garvey asked.

Booker laughed out loud, leaning on the hind legs of the stool at the wooden bar table in his dining room. He bumped his back against the wall behind him. Just under his Publisher's company logo. "Huh? No. I'm for real. I've done everything I ever wanted to do except play quarterback for the Lions. I bat .999, Pop." Booker gloated. "Pure gold."

1: Black Ice

Waking from his sleep to the sound of ice rain. It added layers to an already frozen windshield of Booker's 2020 Chevrolet Tahoe. Peeking through the blinds, he reached for his phone to see if school had been canceled. *Aight nah,* he thought to himself.

Falling into a deep slumber, Booker woke up late into the morning. Opening the refrigerator door, he took out a carton of eggs, turkey sausage, cheese, butter, and almond milk. Reaching into the cupboard, he grabbed a bag of grits, salt, and pepper.

Butter sizzled in the pan, coating the cast iron bottom as it lightly browned. He poured whipped eggs into a smoking skillet. The fan above the stove wasn't loud enough to cancel out the sounds of the first meal of the day.

Fixing his plate, he headed to the bar table of his dining room and turned on the TV. *Prize Fighter Book Trailer II,* he read. Pressing play, he dug his fork into the bottom of his cheese grits. Reaching for his phone, he started typing a text message.

He sent the text before tossing his phone to the couch and added a little more to his newest book. The keyboard typed a metronomes pace at times and a woodpecker's speed during others.

High speed, low speed, a steady ebb, and flow of literature filled the afternoon like the nourishment of his breakfast. *Define nourishment,* he spoke aloud to the Siri feature of his laptop.

After a few hours work on the keys, Booker realized he had done it again. A trail of missed and mixed messages with the lady in his life.

POTUS 2024: BALANCE THE SCALE

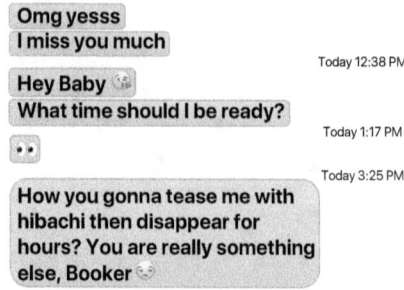

Feeling guilty again, Booker knew it'd be difficult having healthy relationships and two careers. So, he didn't even try. But he couldn't help who he had feelings for. The apple of his eye was starting to sour.

Booker offered in truce, placing his phone on top of the refrigerator. Opening the door, he grabbed a pack of buffalo chicken deli meat, cheddar cheese, tomato slices, lettuce, two pieces of bread, and ranch dressing.

Plating his food, red grapes in hand he took a bite into his sandwich as his brain, stormed. Opening his laptop, ideas flushed into his Microsoft Word App. Continuing work he just departed, more time passed as the day turned night.

Booker went to use the restroom and noticed he misplaced his phone. Flushing the toilet, he dropped a piece of tissue in the trashcan. He washed and dried his hands as he left the bathroom, returning to his seat. Picking up where he left off, he continued his latest manuscript.

Kind of Blue played through the speakers while the *Fresh Prince of Bel-Air* streamed in the background on mute. Finally finishing for the moment, he blew out the candles burning on the TV stand. *Alexa, pause.* He commanded.

Turning up the volume to the television, he returned to the refrigerator for a glass of 100% Ocean Spray cranberry juice. Pouring a glass, he opened the freezer for a large ice cube when he saw his phone sitting atop the stainless steel.

Remembering his last conversation, Booker hit the screen's power button and thumbed through his missed alerts once again. Shaking his head, Booker packed an overnight bag, sprayed his boots, started his truck remotely, hoping to make things better. He replied to Lina's messages and reached for his keys.

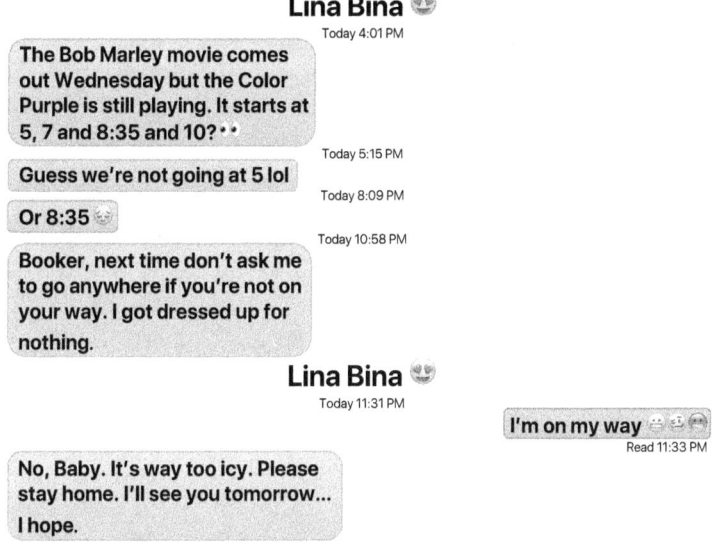

Ignoring her words, he left the skyrise, locking the door behind him. Booker exited the building closest to the parking lot and surveyed the scenery. The ground glistened with the streetlights dancing off of its icy overlay. The trees had ice crystals hanging and falling from them.

The temperature was starting to rise and a steady stream of water began running downhill. Sliding across the parking lot, Booker's feet never raised from the ice-covered asphalt. The downward slope of the hill carried his momentum from door to door. *Should I stay here?* He thought to himself. *I'll be aight.*

Turning on the windshield wipers, a wave of water slid across the warmed glass. Rolling down the windows to the truck, he attempted to speed up the thawing process. Sheets of ice slid across his windows as he switched gears.

Slowly pulling out of the parking lot, he eased to a halt at a stop sign. His truck continued to slide as he quickly thought about turning around. *I hope speed bumps can stop a truck,* he thought to himself, as he carefully drove towards the exit at the main road.

Leaving his condominium, he could only think of his approach to soothing things after his arrival. Slowing to a stop twenty yards before the red light, Booker's truck carried its momentum through the light as it turned green. Wiping his brow, Booker put his hands down from the horn that was seconds away from sounding.

Shaking his head, he drove less than twenty miles per hour the entire trip across town. Signaling into the driveway of a two-bedroom nude, ranch style, wooden house. Pressing the button on the doorbell camera, Booker waited patiently for a reply.

"Use your key," a soft voice said, through the intercom.

"Yes, ma'am." He saluted the screen.

"You are so silly." She laughed as the device went silent.

Stepping inside the warm, fuzzy living room. The plush features warmed Booker from head to toe as he hung up his wet coat. The wheat nubuck material on his Timberland boots were one of the only things still dry on his body. The water repellant he used before his departure kept his Honolulu blue and silver socks toasty too.

Moving slowly across the soft carpet of the hallway in the dark, he washed his hands in the half bathroom. Then walked further down the hall. Knocking on the door of the master bedroom, he undressed himself and got in bed with his lady friend.

Kissing the back of her neck, she wiggled her hips on his, acknowledging his presence. "My bad, ion know what happened. I can't even lie to you. I was in the zone. It ain't as easy to write as it used to be. It comes and goes like Robert Townsend in Meteor Man after he started losing his powers."

"What?" She laughed.

"You never saw Meteor Man?"

"No." She giggled.

"You missed out on an important movie from our childhood."

"I guess."

Pillow talked they did, until it stopped in favor of other things. Starting the morning with a trip to the bathroom, Booker smelled breakfast was in the works. "Smells good in here!" He exclaimed, closing the bathroom door.

Exiting the washroom, he bumped against the wall, recapturing his balance. "*You* should be cooking *me* breakfast after what you put me through yesterday," the pretty lady said.

"That's why I put you through what I did... early this morning." He smiled, flirtatiously.

"You're so badd." She blushed,

"Who's Badd!?" Booker emulated a Michael Jackson dance move. "I apologize, honest. Honest I do." He echoed like the background singer of a group. "Because I know I was wrong."

"First Michael Jackson, now Anita Baker. Who's next? Gotta be 2Pac," she said.

"Makaveli in this." Booker shrugged.

"Here we go again," she said, with a soft, raspy voice.

"DMX!? See, finally you understand how easy it is to talk in bars and movie quotes." He laughed, grabbing hold of her from behind. Walking over to the couch, they sat and watched movies into the afternoon.

"Alright, Lina. I'm getting ready to head on back. You can come by later if you want but dreams don't chase themselves."

Dressed in disappointment, Lina sat up so Booker could remove his arm from around her. Attitude crept over her face and eventually covered her body. "In other words, see you this weekend, talk to you in a few days and I'll get your replies to my texts during the week.

Booker looked stunned. His patterns had become a routine that he'd become unaware of. It wasn't much he could say in response at the moment, being so blindsided from her response. Kissing her forehead, he gathered his belongings and left out the door.

The drive back across town seemed longer than normal as he thought about his last conversation. Turning on the radio, the Traffic Jam Show was going back and forth about the latest remarks from one of the country's most polarizing figures:

The 45th president of the United States of America, Donald Trump is back in the news. He says black voters relate to him because both have been discriminated against. Here's what he had to say, "A lot of people said that's why the Black people like me, because they have been hurt so badly and discriminated against, and they actually viewed me as I'm being discriminated against."

Booker shook his head at the news from his speakers. "Call Manny." He commanded his phone's Siri feature. It was connected to his truck's Bluetooth.

Calling Manny.

"Manny, what's good?"

"I can't call it. What up wit you, bro?"

"I'm running for president this year, brodie."

"Here you go with that shit again." Manny laughed. "You've been talking about that since college."

"I'm serious. Dead ass. I wanted you and Dame to run in college. I just wanted to be y'all Campaign Manager. But if y'all don't want to then shiiit, sign me up, Coach!"

"You're hilarious, bro." Manny laughed hysterically.

"I'm for real!" Booker shouted again, smiling from it all.

"Ay, you'd be a better candidate than everyone else. You've been teaching for a while now. You're an author. You just got your Masters. What else do they want from you, dawg? Shit, you got my vote."

"My man! I'm going to do it for real. It'll be a publicity stunt to sell some books. But shit, if I win, I'll accept. I was just calling to see if you wanted to be a Cabinet Member, Campaign Manager, Advisor, or *something*? The way I see it is, things can't get any worse... I hope. So why not?"

"You ain't never lied. Ay, *you know* I'm in," Manny laughed. "You always trying to do some impossible shit. Remember in college, you tried to walk on water because it was frozen on the top and you fell in the Valley Pond before class?" Manny laughed at the memory he was living in.

"Ay, I had to *at least* try." Booker joked. "I was in class, smelling like fish ass."

The men continued to catch up on old times until Booker reached his destination. "Alright man, I'm going to work on my campaign speeches. Next time I call, it's for real, bro."

"Bet," Manny replied. "Peace."

"Peace!"

The drive across town was more like an obstacle course. Frozen roads from the day before turned into puddles of water. They held Booker's attention as he drove towards the hill.

Arriving at his condo, he began brainstorming ideas to himself. *I need a map,* he thought, walking to his home office. Logging onto his computer, he printed out a detailed map of the state of Michigan. *If I sell 6,670 novels a month for ten months, that puts me over a million dollars. 10,000 short stories and children's books a month is a million over ten months,* he thought.

Booker began drawing outlines around the map for each county and wrote *6,670/10,000* inside of each shape. *Eighty-three counties, times 6,670/10,000 is eight to sixteen million dollars plus,* he calculated mentally. Distracted from his work, he was moved by the voice streaming on his television.

Go into any inner city neighborhood and folks will tell ya, that government alone can't teach our kids to learn. They know that parents have to teach. That children can't achieve unless we raise their expectations and turn off the television sets. And eradicate the slander that says a black youth with a book is acting white. They know those things!

"Yessir!" Booker shouted, saluting at the television. Barack Obama's 2004, Democratic National Convention speech played until the video player recommended another one of his speeches. Booker reached for a tan notebook that was wrapped shut with an elastic band attached to the back of it.

His name and the Publishing House he signed with were printed on the cover in courier font. Jotting down notes in the pad, he studied speeches all night into the early morning. Booker was asleep on the living room couch when his alarm sounded. Wiping his face, he stretched, capped his pen, and got ready for the workday.

11: What's a Debit Card?

"It's time to grow up, 5th graders. It's February." Booker spoke to the class. "Why do you all think I ask you to raise your hand with questions instead of walking up to me?"

Five hands shot up right away and two additional hands rose slowly like the Sun. A chair slid against the carpeted floor, crashing against the table behind it as eleven-year-old, Thompson Steward fell to the floor with his hand still raised. "I know!"

"You clearly don't know how to raise your hand, *quietly*," Booker said with his eyebrows, high as the sky. "But Emajean sure does. Yes?" He gestured with an open palm.

"Because if one of us walks up to you, other students will think it's OK too. The next thing you know, it'll be half the class at your desk."

"Bingo!" Booker pointed at the little girl. "I couldn't have said it any better. That's actually exactly what I said. What else?"

"It's quicker to raise your hand," a husky boy answered, sitting front row center. His smile often brightened the room without a light.

"If they know that, word for word almost. Why don't *some* of you?" He looked at the culprits, calmly circling the room. "Think about that when you reflect in your journals later." After a little wait time, he said, "Get ready for Math, the timer is set for one minute. Don't get ready in a minute, be ready in a minute."

Booker Garvey III ran a tight ship inside room 505. He expected nothing short of their best. Students of many different backgrounds and ethnicities entered his class a 5th grader and left ready for 7th grade. "Alright, the dividend means what?"

"The total number!" Many students shouted.

"Good, what about the divisor?" He asked, mid review.

"The amount that makes an even group!" More answered routinely.

"Better…" Pausing dramatically, he assigned a problem. "What is the quotient of four hundred thirteen divided by seven?" He posed to the class. "Show your answer as a fraction and a remainder."

Silence crept over the room. "Have an answer in four minutes. Get busy."

The timer beeped thrice as the clock started. Pencils zipped across papers on the tables, documenting history in the making. Seconds into the assignment, one student seemed puzzled.

"You dumb," one boy said to another.

"Hey, hey, hey! Watch that d-word." Booker's deep voice boomed. "What makes you think it's OK to insult someone for struggling? I struggle writing with my left hand, does that make me the d-word?" Booker asked.

"No…" the boy dragged out.

"Alright then, leave that young man alone and get your work done. But first, you need to apologize."

"I apologize, Greg."

"It's alright."

"Ninety seconds." Booker reminded the class.

"Done!" One shouted.

"If you finish early, check your work. Divisor times the whole groups in the quotient plus the remainder. If you get the divided, your answer is right."

Picking up her pencil, Alice continued the assignment, while her neighbor struggled greatly. "DMSBR. You already divided, multiply!" She said, impatiently.

"Alice, relax. Otherwise let me or someone else help her. Ten seconds." Booker updated the class. "Three, two, one. Times up."

Beep! Beep! Beep!

"How many sevens are in four?"

"One!" Thompson answered confidently.

"One—" the class echoed slowly.

"Think before you speak, don't just repeat after someone else. All of you who said one were wrong. But the one person who took their time and answered last in row three is absolutely right. Great job, Elliott. Zero."

"That's what I thought," one boy said.

"Then say it." Booker encouraged, moving on to the next question. "Think before you answer. How many sevens are in forty-one?"

5!

6!

5!

6!

"Don't argue, prove it." Taping his fingers with a pencil, the class counted by seven as he touched each finger.

7, 14, 21, 28, 35, 42—

"Stop, too much. What's the answer?"

5!

Finishing the problem with the class, it was their time to work. "Fifty-nine is correct. What does the quotient mean in this problem?" He wondered before the bell.

"There's fifty-nine groups of seven if we use four hundred thirteen things." Thompson answered confidently.

"Bingo!" Booker fist bumped Thompson. I'm looking for groups who are ready. When I see you, I will call you."

Having lined up the students, out the door they went as Booker followed behind them. While students left the building for recess, Booker went down the hall to talk to his mentor. "What's up third graders?" He asked, entering Mrs. Taft's room.

"Hi, Mr. Garvey," they replied in unison.

"Wassup, LT?"

"Hey Garvey. How was the weekend?"

"It was smooth, fast. My Pop was in town for the Superbowl. That game was crazy! Mahomes got three of them thangs now. I watched it thirty minutes late for the Lions not making it. I was still a lil mad about them losing to San Francisco." Booker shook his head. Looking down at his division championship T-Shirt, he grabbed it in a ball, living in anguish all over again.

"Oh yeah. I decided to run for president this year too."

Laughing, Mrs. Taft couldn't believe her ears and completely disregarded his announcement. "The boys are in town. I told them you golf now. They want to go with you when the weather breaks."

"I don't know if I'm ready to golf with them. They're a sneeze away from the pros."

"Yeah." She blushed.

"We can hit the driving range. I have tee time later today. I go every Tuesday. Tell them to meet me up there."

Continuing to catch up on the extended weekend, Booker let Mrs. Taft in on a few more things. "You know these young'ns do hard drugs now? I'm talking crack. Probably because they never saw crackheads. Growing up in the '90s, we saw them too much in HP. Way too much, LT."

Leora Taft grew up in the south. Where she was widely known as the great granddaughter of an original Freedom Hunter. Her family knew their lineage and passed it down from generation to generation. Originally from Florida, Her story was a lot different than Booker's. Trauma was present in both situations even if they failed to realize it themselves.

"OK, I'll text them after I drop the class off for Art."

"Cool."

Exiting the room, he looked at a student's work on his way out and had a double take. "If I were president…" Booker held the young man's assignment as he read it aloud.

"Who would you want to be your vice president?" Booker mumbled to himself, continuing to read the youngster's work. "Barack Obama!?" He exclaimed. "That's not a bad idea." Booker pulled his chin hair post thought. Then gave the youngster a fist bump on his way out of the room.

As he left for the parking lot, Booker had to make a call for the sake of time.

Ring, ring, ring.

"Jetto Sushi, how can I help you?"

"Hi, can I get a Crunch Toba Roll?"

"Anything else?"

"That's it."

"OK, give us fifteen minutes."

Jumping into his V8, Chevrolet Tahoe, Booker took off down Stadium drive arriving at his destination. As soon as he walked into the establishment, he stopped at the mini station by the door. Where he picked up chopsticks and soy sauce before walking to the counter to get his order. Booker placed his utensils inside a plastic bag. Reaching for the order with his name written across the top, a piece of eye candy caught his attention.

Booker couldn't see much, but she was appealing from behind as she exited the building. He could only wonder what would've happened if he arrived a little earlier. Her scent left a trail, but she had already departed by the time he got outside.

Returning from lunch, Booker sat at his desk, clutching his phone in one hand. He was watching the *Prize Fighter Book Trailer I* with chopsticks in the other hand.

"Mr. Garvey, I hate to bother you on your lunch break, but your class is out of control. They aren't listening to anybody," Ms. Lehman, the lunchroom aide said. Having made her way down to his classroom.

"Here we go." Booker set off down the hall. "What are they doing? Loud? Who is it?"

"Being disrespectful, yelling, play fighting. It's getting hard to tell if they're playing or serious."

Shaking his head, Booker could hear noise coming from the cafeteria over ten yards out.

"Are they like this, every day?"

"Not every day. Once or twice a week. Sometimes none."

The noise from the cafeteria bounced off the wall perpendicular to the entrance, echoing in the halls. "Why are you all so loud?" Booker asked a silent lunchroom. "Now, you know how to be quiet?" He paused his speech to survey the room and looked them all in the eyes.

"Do the right thing because you expect it from yourself. Not because you saw me. Line up and stop at the door." He motioned forward towards the classroom as they exited the cafeteria.

The class walked, silently. They were confused by how fast things turned. One second everything was great. Conversations turned into jokes; jokes led to challenges and challenges meant consequences.

"Why did Ms. Lehman come get me in the middle of my lunch?" Booker asked, entering the classroom. "Because when I walked in, you all looked like the Class of the Year."

"We were loud," one student answered.

"Obviously. But that doesn't answer my question, at all." Booker replied, squinting eyes that were decorated with disappointment. "The question was why did she come get me in the middle of my sushi?"

"What kind of sushi did you have today, Mr. Garvey, shrimp tempura?" A little girl asked with a tilted head, wondering.

"Crunch Toba roll. But that *still* doesn't answer my question, Amanee." Booker countered, looking at a pile of morning work papers that had been thrown on the counter.

"I asked you all to put your papers in a pile, people. It's February." Two boys quickly fixed the stack. "Thanks, row three for straightening that up. Row one, that was on you. Row two followed your lead and row three got things done. Three points for row three." Booker walked behind his desk, reaching for a navy blue, dry erase maker. Adding points to the scoreboard, he recognized they took the lead.

Yes!

Let's go!

"Row three, wins. Game ends at twenty-five. Well, twenty-six today." Booker shrugged. "Row three, come on up and pick your prize. Row one and two, clean out your desks. Get ready to move."

Booker walked over to the coat closet by the door to get a large, black box full of prizes that had been donated from stores around the city. "200k VC?! Get out of here!" One boy shouted.

"You're right. Get out of here, Jose. I need that—," Kaynile said, dragging out his thoughts, moving things around in the wooden box. "Fifty-dollar PlayStation Store gift card in my life right now." He grinned.

"Puh-leez, I'll take the manicures for two! Me and Mommy are going out for breakfast and mani's this weekend. Absolutely." Jasmine looked at her fingernails, prissily.

Thanks, Mr. Garvey!

"You earned it." Booker saluted the winning group. "Row one and two, line up. When I call your name, start moving into your new desks. Row three, you have a little free time until they're ready to move on," Booker informed the champions. "If any of you want to switch seats, now is the time to get in line." No one budged.

While the class got ready to move, Booker reached for a white and green cylinder full of cleaning wipes. "After you clean your desk, wash your hands and get ready for Writing."

While students finished moving into their new desks, it was time to start over fresh. "Alright, one minute. Be ready for

POTUS 2024: BALANCE THE SCALE

Writing. Don't get ready in a minute. Be ready in a minute," Booker urged. Setting up the document camera, he showed his notebook to the class.

Beep! Beep! Beep!

Beep. Stopping the timer, Booker began to sign his name in the top right-hand corner on the right page of his wire bound, spiral notebook. Writing his name and date to both of the opened pages, he began to address the class.

"Alright, open your notebook to, two clean sheets. Make sure your name and date are in the top right-hand corner on both pages. Think about if a page falls out of your notebook. Or when we needed to flip to November 10th of last year, yesterday; to read your Free Choice Friday journals. Most of the class made some of you look bad just by dating their pages." Booker started receiving immediate reinforcement.

"Ooooh," Thompson said, covering his mouth.

"Yup!" Jose smiled.

"Make sure to date this page. We will be coming back to it. That's a guarantee, people." He pointed upwards.

Booker didn't sugarcoat much for his students. Middle school was coming soon. A tall task it could be for the unprepared. Knowing so, Booker kept it very honest with his students. "Three million, nine hundred thousand. That's about how many 5th graders there are in the country. I'm not saying this to scare you. I'm saying this to prepare you."

Booker was a motivator, and he did so with truth. The way he saw it, certain truths were so ugly, they had to be corrected. "I've done everything I've ever tried. Except play quarterback for the Lions and even that, I know why it didn't happen..."

"Why you like the Lions so much, Mr. Garvey? They didn't even want you." Mavin needed answers.

"I never said they didn't want me. I said... I played with or against three people who went pro. The two I played with taught me why I didn't make it." Booker was prepared to clear the air.

"Because you was weak?" Thompson asked, laughing.

"Nah, Mr. Garvey got an arm. I used to see him throw the ball all the time, last year," Ramon replied.

"I was alright." Booker nodded, pulling the chin hairs of his beard. "I scored a couple times and got my tackles." He nodded again. "But I was a hitter. So, I didn't talk much. If somebody called me weak like Thompson just did."

Booker pointed at Thompson. "*Blow the whistle, Coach!* I used to always yell."

The boys laughed as he went on. "I never got a pick or a sack but besides that, I was satisfied. I guess. I didn't like the way it ended, at all." Booker answered, living in a memory.

"I don't know what Brandon Graham did to go pro but we scrimmaged them, seven on seven when I was at Highland Park, and he was at Crockett. Then I had to switch schools and it was over. They didn't have a team." Booker shrugged, shaking his head.

"Greenwood and Rock went pro because they stayed after practice running with tires and parachutes on their back. Hitting the sleds and running agility drills… in the dark. The only light was Coach's high beams on his truck.

"I didn't go pro because I hopped on my bike and went home after practice. I didn't lift weights until I was grown except for leg day. I had hops so I never skipped leg day.

"But I was lifting PlayStation and Nintendo 64 controllers instead of studying, lifting books!" He shouted, curling a pair of textbooks like dumbbells. Looking left to right, he read from two opened books as his arms alternated up and down.

The class quietly laughed then Booker said, "Point is, I should probably tell Radioshack no more gaming gift cards; since they distracted *me* so much, huh?"

Yesss!

Nooo!

The girls and boys went back and forth like Tug of War before being distracted by a quick, snap-clap pattern.

Clap, clap, snap, snap, clap. Snap
Clap, clap, snap, snap, clap. Snap

After repeating the cadence, Booker steered the lesson back on track. "Alright, back to the lesson. Name and date, make sure it's in the top, right hand corner. On the left page, write *High School Jobs* in a bubble in the center of the page. Now, Attach some jobs you might want to have in high school to that bubble."

The class grew quiet, unsure of where to start. "I worked at Subway and McDonald's my junior and senior year of high

POTUS 2024: BALANCE THE SCALE

school. But my first job was a summer job at Highland Park Community College when I was fourteen."

Amanee raised her hand. "Yes?" Booker nodded her way.

"My mom worked at Macy's in high school. She said it was called Hudson's back then."

"Sure was. I remember Hudson's. That's what it was called when I was in 5th grade." Booker smiled. "They had some really good chocolate chunk cookies in their bakery. It was Marshall Field's for a little while before Macy's." He jogged his memory.

I wanna work at TJ Maxx when I get to high school. It looks fun.

Costco. They got Big ol juices.

Red Lobster!

Ummm, I wanna work at Red Lobster too. Just for the biscuits.

Them biscuits good

Ideas swarmed the class like a hornet's nest. "When you all get to high school, especially if you have siblings, you're going to cost your parents a lot of money and you need to help out by buying things for yourself like we did."

I buy my own food at the store sometimes

I bought this T-shirt

I buy my own candy

"I'm talking about real stuff. Once I got to 11th and 12th grade, I was buying my own clothes and shoes. My cousin worked at Foot Action and he used to get our Jordan's sometimes. I only had the Space Jams but my brother used to get a lot of shoes. That was my cousin's high school job too by the way."

Booker raised his eyebrows asking, "Why might someone need a job in high school?"

To pay a car lease?

"If you're lucky. Most high schoolers have used cars that are paid for. I had a '92 Buick Regal. Roxanne was her name. It drove like a boat on wheels. I got her the last week of high school before graduation. But yes, if you have a car, a job definitely makes things easier. What else?"

Credit cards?

"Probably not. You have to be eighteen to get a credit. But maybe! If you're eighteen."

"My cousin got a credit card and he's only sixteen." Thompson blurted out.

"Your cousin has a debit card. Unless someone added him to their account. Does anyone know the difference between a debit card and a credit card?"

"Yea," Thompson answered while the class hesitated.

"What's a debit card?" Booker asked, opening the floor.

"It's a card that lets you buy stuff." He rubbed his chin.

"Yes, but so does a credit card," Booker countered.

"It's a card that you get to buy stuff. Then you pay it back later?" He asked a question with his tone.

"Not quite. That's a credit card, good. So, what's a debit card?"

"Your money?" He answered, unsurely.

"Bingo," Booker replied, seeing it as the simplest form of the answer. "Yes, that's exactly what it is. A debit card is linked to a checking account which is the money you put into the bank.

"A credit card is a loan on a card pretty much. You get a certain amount and make payments on it if you spend anything. Credit card companies make their money off of interest. Interest means you pay a piece of what you owe in fees. Remember decimals?"

Yeah!

"Interest is a percentage like decimals. Anything that says 29.99% interest means $29.99 in fees for everyone hundred dollars you owe, per year. That's called APR. Annual Percentage Rate. Write that down on the list of things I told you all to never forget, A-P-R," Booker paused Writing for a Life Skills lesson.

"Dang!" Thompson shouted.

"That's almost a third," Jose added. While adding three letters to a running list on the back cover of his notebook.

"How much is one third as a decimal?" He asked the class.

Pointing at the boy seated by the window, he called on, "Ramon?"

"About thirty-three and thirty-three hundredths?"

"Say it like you mean it." Booker replied, walking his way with his eyebrows coming together.

"Thirty-three and thirty-three hundredths." Ramon's increased confidence spoke volumes.

"Bingo!" Booker dropped off a strip of raffle tickets on Ramon's desk to use as currency in the class store.

Concluding his mini lesson, Booker said, "Alright, back to the lecture at hand. Why else would a high schooler need a job?"
Food
Snacks
Toys
"You all are thinking like 5th graders. I need you all to think like high schoolers. At least 8th graders." He joked. "When you all get older, you're going to want to do things like go to the movies with your friends."
Yup!
"Or go to the mall with your friends. You have to buy your own video games if that's your thing. When you get older, you get dressed up and go to dances. What are those called? Who knows?"
Prom!
Homecoming!
My sister goes to Prom this year.
"Bingo! You'll have to pay for dresses, rent tuxedos, and boys, you're going to have to buy your prom date's food and corsage. That's the flower they wear."

Laughs from the boys made the girls snicker at the weight of their responsibility. "Yassss, get what you deserve," Amanee replied.

Booker covered a laugh under his breath with a question, "What else?"
Help with the bills
"If you're responsible," Booker said. Adding supporting ideas to his bubble map on the document camera, the white board displayed his writing. Students repeated their answers until they were written down.
Buy a pet
"If the people at home let you."
Change the oil
"We'll say *car maintenance.*"
Get gas
Buy gifts
Pay my phone bill
"I've definitely been paying my phone bill since I was sixteen. Alright, sounds like you all have a good idea of what I mean. Write at least three paragraphs. Think about where you'd want to work in high school." Booker held up his first finger.

"Why you'd want to work there and what you'd do with the money. Write at least one paragraph about each of the three." Booker held up three fingers on his left hand while writing the prompts right-handed. "Any questions?" He asked

No one raised their hand or said a thing until Booker said, "Alright, talk amongst yourselves, give each other some ideas. When the timer beeps, it's just you and those pages. Five minutes, get busy." At an instant, chatter swirled around the class with excitement.

Beep! Beep! Beep!

The fourth *Beep!* Stopped the timer. "Alright, level zero. Get busy…" Booker prompted, adjusting the clock. "Twenty minutes. If you finish early, reread your work to make sure you said what you meant to say and not what you thought you said.

"I read my books anywhere between five to ten times before they're published. I'm sure. I read my first book at least fifty times. Maybe not all at once but in sections, for sure. Thoughts move quicker than your fingers," he reminded them.

"How long it take to write yo books, Mr. Garvey?" Thompson asked, pencil in hand.

"About three to four months then another six months to a year to edit them. I'm writing a live book now that I'm challenging myself to finish writing the day after Election Day, November fifth. Then release it eight months later on July 5, 2025. That gives me a little under a year and a half. You all will be headed to 7th grade when it comes out.

"I'm going to *show* you all how to reach a goal and not just set one," Booker informed the class. "I'm not even going to *think* about, *what if I don't finish in time*. Nope! That's not how I think. I'm *going* to make it happen and if I don't, I'll deal with it in November. Until then I have nine months to finish, and I can't finish this one early. The story doesn't end until the day after Election Day."

"What's it called?" Thompson asked, locked in.

"POTUS 2024."

"Can I get a copy?"

"Not this time. This one is for your parents. You have to wait until you're eighteen. Just like those credit cards."

III: Follow Me!

Seventy-seven miles per hour read the dashboard to Booker's 2020 Chevrolet Tahoe. Booker coasted down I-94 East for a quick trip home to see his family over the weekend. Exiting the freeway for M-10 North, he made a detour to pick up a surprise dinner for his favorite girl. "Can I help you?" The cashier asked.

"How you doing? Can I get a beef patty, two large jerk chicken dinners? One with cabbage, the other with greens and as much dressing on the rice that you can give me." He smiled, removing his wallet from his back pocket. The smell of the food reminded him of high school. The Jamaican restaurant had satisfied his appetite for years on in. The spices from the pots brewing in the back tickled his nose and widened his eyes. "Could you make that four dinners? I'm going to go with greens and mixed vegetables for the last two, please and two chicken patties?"

The server closed out the order, squinting her eyes to see the numbers on the register. She was a middle-aged Jamaican woman with an apron stained with food prepared by the soul. "Sixty-eight, ninety." The woman totaled on the register. Booker inserted his debit card into the card reader, entered his pin number, and ended the transaction.

Reaching into his wallet, he pulled out a ten-dollar bill and dropped it in the tip jar. "Thanks." She smiled, pushing her glasses up her nose.

After a brief wait, the woman bagged everything and handed it to Booker over the counter. "Thanks so much, have a great day." The woman waved goodbye.

"Yes, ma'am. You too, thanks." Booker smelled the food through the bag. Unable to practice patience, he removed the beef patty, devouring it on the way to his truck. Riding down West

McNichols towards Wyoming, Booker's flashbacks continued, being in his high school stomping ground.

Passing Marygrove College then the University of Detroit Mercy, he was doused in memories. One of them stared at him live in the flesh. Slowing to a halt at the stoplight, Booker bulged his eyes at the woman crossing the street with her school aged son. Seeing who she was, he could only wonder, what if? Picking up the little boy's hat that had fallen out of his pocket, she put her hand up to thank the driver for waiting.

Realizing who she was locked eyes with, her mouth opened and momentarily, she couldn't move. A tug from the boy snapped her back into reality. With blushed cheeks, she smiled at Booker, refreshed her curls, and went on her way. As the light turned green, Booker followed her with his eyes while she walked down the street to her residence.

"The good ol days." He whispered to himself as she picked up the little boy's hat again across the street. The woman looked back, caught Booker's eye, and waved. Booker honked his horn in unison with the car behind him. Smiled, waved, took his foot off the brake, and drove to Detroit's Eastside.

Music blared from the speakers from Hip Hop, R&B, to Soul Music from the 1970s. "Nobody's interested in learning, but the teacher!" Booker sang along as the band played on.

Segregation, determination, demonstration, integration, aggravation, humiliation, obligation to our nation. Ball of confusion.... that's what the world is today. Hey, hey!

His truck zoomed across the railroad tracks unphased as his *Road Trip Playlist* continued. "God said he should send his one begotten son to lead the wild into the ways of the man... follow me!" Booker shouted, riding down McNichols.

The radio continued to blast until the engine powered off and the door opened. Holding the food with two hands for safety measures, he walked up the wooden stairs greeted by a very familiar face. "Hey Ma!" He shouted with animation as he walked through the opened door, kissing her cheek.

Her honey brown skin complimented the gold shirt she sported from her most recent class reunion. "Is this for me?" She asked, pleasantly surprised.

"Of course! You already know I gotta hit Caribbean Citchen when I'm in the city. How you be?!"

"Good!" She smiled. "Even better now."

"That's what I'm talking about!" Making a trip to the restroom to wash his hands, he had a seat on the couch to check on the game before fixing a plate. "Did the Pistons win?" He asked.

"Not this time. They'll be better next year," she predicted.

Laughing, he stood to his feet to eat. "I hope you're right, Ma. I just got season tickets. They were so low, I had to."

"I'm scared to ask."

"I'm scared to tell." He laughed. "You coming to a game with me?"

"Nooo, I can see just fine from here."

"Aw c'mon nah, Ma!" Booker got animated.

"If Steph and Cade are playing, maybe." She considered.

"I'll take it! I'll let you know when I get em!"

"Oh, Lord. What did I get myself into?"

"A good ol time! What you mean?" He laughed. "I'ma get my plate before it gets cold on me." Walking to the kitchen, he stopped to stare at the Family Tree portraits on the wall from his great-great grandparents down to the newest additions of the family tree, his nieces and nephew.

"We're still waiting on the pitter pats of feet from you."

"I bet." Reminding her, "You know what I say. I have the rest of my life to worry about the rest of my life."

"That's what you say. What about Shantel? Could you see yourself marrying her?"

"Aw, Ma. We broke up like five years ago." Booker thought aloud, remembering their timeline. "Right before the pandemic."

"My bad." She laughed. "I can't keep up with you *and* your brother after all these years."

"Lina." Booker reminded her.

"Lina. I knew that. I like Lina."

"Good." Booker chuckled. "I don't know, Ma. I have a lot I'm trying to do before I settle down because I want to be the best dad and father of all time!" He said with his fists up, bouncing back and forth, mocking Muhammad Ali. "I can't do that right now with these goals of mine."

"You are definitely the dreamer who never woke up, which is good. Stay that way as long as you can. Too many people limit themselves to their current situation. That's one thing I will say about you. Whatever you want to do, you find a way to get it done… except for chores when you were growing up."

"I remember you telling me that since I was Callie's age." Booker laughed, holding his stomach. "Did I tell you my next outlandish story of triumph?"

"Uh oh, no. But I'm ready for whatever it is."

"Forty-Seven," he replied.

"You're not even forty. You can do whatever you set your mind to. I've always told you that. But aging expeditiously isn't one of them, Son. Didn't your uncle tell you to *Slow down little brother. Don't be in a hurry to grow up.*" She used a deep voice to mock her brother-in-law.

"Every time I see him." Booker laughed at her impression. "Nope, no time machines here. I'll give you one guess."

"An outlandish story of triumph?" She pondered. "I don't know, man. What, run for president?"

"How'd you know!?"

"Know what?"

"I'm running for president."

"President of what?"

"President of The United States." He chuckled. "POTUS."

"For what?!" She exclaimed with peaked curiosity.

"It's a publicity stunt to sell some books. I'm writing a live book about it now. It's a story about the election and I'm releasing it on the 5th of July 2025. It's called POTUS 2024."

"July 5th? Why not the 4th?"

"Election Day is 11/5. Eight months later is 7/5. Eleven, seven. Seven, eleven." He moved his hands up and down with the two numbers. "Those are lucky numbers."

"Seven is the number of completion. Five is my favorite. I got three or four reasons, Ma." He chuckled. "You know how I am with numbers. LOTT drops it a day early though. So, it kinda comes out on the 4th."

"I got ya." She laughed. "What if you win?"

"I haven't thought about that yet." Booker shrugged.

IV: Balance the Scale

As time continued to pass with the westerlies, Booker was getting more organized and added several suits and blazers to his wardrobe. He even bought a tuxedo for election night. Win, lose, or draw. He was ready to make a splash in the world and it all started Thursday, April 25, 2024. Which was only eight days away.

"17.5," the tailor said. Her assistant scribbled numbers on a sheet of paper. Booker's shirt measurements were being taken. "All right, we're all done here. We'll be making alterations through Friday. You can pick up your pants and blazer anytime Saturday," the woman instructed.

"Perfect!" Booker pumped his fist. "OK, see you then. Thanks."

Exiting Kalamazoo Custom Tailoring along The Kalamazoo Mall, Booker walked through a market. It took him to the back of the buildings where he parked. Removing his phone from his jacket pocket, he thumbed through his contacts until he found who he was looking for. "Hey, Lady."

"Hey, Big Head."

"I'm leaving the tailor. I had to pick up my tuxedo for election night and my suit for my presidential announcement. You know my election campaign starts on Earth Day, right? I announce it on the 25th."

"You were serious about that? I thought you were just venting." She giggled.

"When have you known me to vent without action? Venting without action is a waste of time," he continued. "And I try my damndest not to waste time."

"Tell me about it."

"You hungry? I'm headed to Olive Garden for a presidential feast! I'm eating for the country." Booker grinned.

Laughing, she listed her order. "Chicken tortellini and lasagna frittas please?" She requested.

"No shrimp?"

"Are you getting shrimp?"

"You know it," Booker said without doubt.

"Sure. Me too," she added.

Booker placed a call-in order and rehearsed his presidential address voice on the way to the restaurant. *My fellow Americans,* "Ahem!" He cleared his throat. *MY FELLOW AMERICANS!* He shouted. "Nah, way too much." Booker chuckled to himself. "My fellow Americans," he said, confidently. Shaking his head up and down, it was apparent Booker found his presidential tone.

Arriving early to the restaurant, he backed into a carryout spot marked with the number seven. Opening the center console, he removed a notebook and pencil then began to write his presidential announcement speech. Licking the corner of his mouth for concentration, he wrapped it up by yelling, "We need to balance the scale!"

Smiling from ear to ear, his writing process had officially ended as the waitress knocked on his window, grinning. She was in her early thirties with a curvy waist and a beautiful smile. Ones, fives, tens, twenties, and a fifty-dollar bill were pinned on her apron. It was covered in Italian herbs and sauces.

"How you doing?" Booker asked, greeting the woman.

"Good, you?" She handed Booker an oversized bag and receipt book through the window.

"Even better now." Smelling the food inside the bag, he said, "Y'all did it this time!"

"I'll let the kitchen staff know." She smiled.

"Thanks, and Happy birthday!" Booker said. "It is your birthday, right?" He asked, writing on the restaurant's copy of the receipt.

"I graduate from Western next Saturday." The woman snickered. "Today's my last day."

"Aw, shit. Congrats!"

"Thank you."

Booker slid her a twenty-dollar bill folded over his business card to add to her collection.

"Theirs is on the receipt. That's for you." He nodded, licking his bottom lip.

"Wowww, thanks. Have a nice niiight." She waved, walking towards the restaurant.

"Thanks. You too." Booker sent a text message as he switched gears and pulled out of the parking lot.

Lina Bina 😜
Today 5:54 PM

I'm on my way
Delivered

Booker's business card slipped through the fold of the bill and fell to the ground. Surprised, she quickly picked it up. Blushing as he drove away, she added them both to her unpinned tips inside her fanny pack.

Cruising down the street of a familiar location, the wooden ranch welcomed his arrival with a vacant spot in the driveway. Exiting his truck, he grabbed the big bag of food as he walked to the front door. Pressing the doorbell, he was greeted with a familiar line, "Use your key."

"Yes ma'am," he answered routinely.

Opening the door, he was greeted with a big bear hug and kisses to the lips. "I knew you liked OG, but damn!" He shouted as she undressed him.

The temperature of the living room matched the boxed food in his bag, hot and steamy. As things returned to normal, Lina picked fuzzies from Booker's goatee. "You had me rolling around this muh fucka like Sonic!"

"You are so silly!" She shouted full of ecstasy.

"I'll be that." He smirked, slapping her on the behind.

Grabbing hold of Booker 's hand, she led him to the kitchen for dinner. Preheating the oven to three hundred degrees, she plated each dish. Covered it with a stainless steel lid, set the timer, and closed the oven door.

Grabbing her in his arms, Booker began talking about his future plans. "You're going to make a mighty fine First Lady."

"You are such an old man." She giggled.

"Watch that O-word. I'm still in my mid-thirties, thank *you* very much."

"Umm hmm, thirty-six going on seventy."

"I'll still be good. Our last two presidents were old as shit… to be president." He clarified his statement. "I hope to make it to at least one hundred before I clock out. So, they're not old. They're old to be president. Now get y'all *old to be president* ass on and let me get that spot. Damn!"

Laughing hysterically, Lina found the stability to ask, "So, what are you going to do if you win?"

"People keep asking me that. I don't really know what to say, honestly. I guess I'll accept." Booker sat still, thinking of the many possibilities and how fast things could change at any given moment.

"One thing that I know for certain is that I can't lie to the people. I might withhold information about Aliens and shit like that."

Lina laughed and applied pressure. "Withholding information on Aliens is kinda expected. What *will* you tell us, Mr. President?"

"If I take office and find out America sold all of our land and we're renting land from China, I'm snitching!" He shouted, banging on the tabletop.

"If I find out that the Bilderberg Group or the Federal Reserve owns American land… I'm snitching! When I say owns or sold all our land, I'm talking about states not lots!" He banged on the table again, continuing his thought.

"Student loan relief, raising teacher pay, shortening the workday, and tax cuts for all Americans will be my first four moves. Working with the United Nations about peace talk is fifth.

"We'll build housing projects for the homeless and citizens with low income who don't qualify for government assistance. With daycares and trade skills training *inside* the housing projects. That's sixth, seventh, and eighth.

"Shit, when I get that done, I might go down as the greatest president of all time." Booker thought ahead, holding his chin, looking into the future.

"Yasssss! Who's your running mate?" Lina wondered.

"I don't know… that's my only problem." He replied with a puzzling look on his face.

V: Campaign Announcement

After weeks of preparation, Booker was finally ready to make his Campaign Announcement. In order to do so, he was back on the road to his hometown of Highland Park, Michigan where it all began. "I gotta go to Hart Plaza real quick, you trying to roll?" He asked his brother, Ian.

"For the draft? You know it's packed. Downtown is crazy right now."

"That too. I'm getting ready to make my Campaign Announcement. Only thing is, I forgot my suit." Booker frowned with eyebrows meeting in the middle of his face.

Laughing hysterically, Ian got in line behind everyone who did the same before him.

"Mannn, I'm glad I don't have low self-esteem. Everybody laughs when I say that. Ay, they laughed at B-Rack too!" Booker shouted.

"Not as loud because Barack had political experience. You're a teacher, my guy." Ian reminded him, still chuckling about it all.

"Millard, James, Chester, and Lyndon were all teachers before they became president, Playboy." Booker pounded his chest, yelling, "Let's go!"

"This is why people laugh, Bro." Ian chuckled. "You're a silly dude."

"Kawhi and I prefer *fun guy*." Booker shrugged.

"See what I mean." Ian laughed. "Who quotes Kawhi? He barely talks. I thought he was mute until he laughed that one time."

"Ay, that muh fucka funny. Y'all trip'n. He who laughs first, laughs last. You heard the last laugh during their championship parade. Now, when you hear me laugh all loud and slow n'shit at the Inauguration. Then I wink at the camera, just know it's for this moment reht nah!" Booker shouted.

"You ain't gotta wink at the camera, my guy. I'll be in the front row next to Mom and Pop." He laughed, extending his fist for a pound. "Got my vote."

"My dawg!" Booker smiled, pounding fists.

"I really am about to head to Hart Plaza though, you coming?"

"If it's for the draft, I got better seats at home. If it's for the Campaign Announcement, I'll do it. I'll do it, you know I'll do it!"

"Aight, Samuel L," Booker laughed at the 1990s movie line. "It's smooth, brodie. I'ma hit the draft and announce my campaign a little later. I'ma need that suit!"

"Fasho."

Separating for the moment, Booker and Ian shook hands before parting ways. Walking to the corner, he waited patiently for his Ride Share car service that was on the way to take him Downtown Detroit. Carrying his camera bag and tripod, Booker looked around at the neighborhood that groomed him, reliving his past.

The field where they played football and the driveway next to it that housed their basketball court. They raced in the street. The front yards were their wrestling and sometimes boxing rings. Then the porches that hosted many conversations and activities.

An electric car pulled up to the scene, interrupting his memories as he searched his app to see what color vehicle he was awaiting. Finding who he was looking for, he flagged down the car and got in. "How you doing?" He asked.

"Good." The lady replied in short.

Sitting in the back of the vehicle, Booker opted out of pulling teeth. He removed his phone from his pants pocket and caught up on YouTube videos that he missed driving back to the city. "Get yo stupid ass on. Retarded mutha fucka!" The driver screamed, honking her horn.

"Hmmp," Booker responded, tuning into the Mike Tyson comeback fight press conference. "Once he's in that ring, he has to fight like his life is depending on it... because it will be."

"I love Mike Tyson." The driver announced having heard the video, smiling for the first time."

"Iron Mike is a wild boy!" Booker exclaimed, all in on the press conference.

"Ain't he? He never gave a fuck." She laughed.

"Never!" Booker chuckled.

"Do you want me to see how long it takes for traffic to clear?"

"This is fine, thanks."

Exiting the vehicle, Booker walked through crowds of people. Fan gear flooded the streets with Honolulu blue and silver being the most dominant colors. "It's time Detroit!" Booker yelled with his fists up.

"Yeah!" The people around him rejoiced, cheering loudly and passionately.

"Book!" A voice called from behind him.

"Manny! What's good?!" Booker asked, shaking hands. "I was just about to call you, bro. I *just* got out the Ride Share."

"And already caused a commotion."

"Say brutha, it's our time! What can I say?!" He asked, posing.

"Dyno-Mite!" Manny kept it going.

Laughing, talking, and walking, the two headed towards Campus Martius for the draft day festivities. "There goes Amon Ra St. Brown." Manny pointed.

"Brutha Brown! Where?"

"Over there at the Little Caesars Pizza Toss Station." He pointed as they moved over a few steps.

"Let's go over there," Booker and Manny jogged lightly to the pizza station that had a line longer than the eye could see.

The wide receiver was challenging fans in line while they exited stage left, loss after loss. Manny stepped up to the throwing section and hurled footballs at the pizza shaped targets. Hitting targets close, intermediate, and far away, Manny heard something no one else had. "You're the first person to beat me." He shook Manny's hand.

"Thanks, bruh! Good game. Good luck this season in New Orleans!" Manny said, walking away.

"Yessir! I already booked my flight!" Booker chimed in, dancing like Mike Epps.

He laughed, tapping his heart with his right hand, pointed at them before saluting. Then he started engaging with a younger fan he saw wearing a St. Brown jersey.

"How you do that? I'm the quarterback between the two of us, I thought. You could've been Tim Hiller's backup at Western with that accuracy."

"And if I was 6'4, I would've started," Manny replied.

"I would've played receiver and came back as a walk-on if Four was throwing dimes like that!" Booker shouted.

Crossing Jefferson Avenue, Booker took out a blue, folding megaphone from his backpack. After overhearing a conversation behind him, he was moved to do something about it. "How you do that so fast? Where you get that come from?" Manny laughed hysterically.

"You can find almost anything on the internet, bro. It's 2024. I got it for my Campaign Announcement."

"You were serious?!" Manny asked, finally putting everything together, still laughing from the pit of his solar plexus.

"I can show you better than I can tell you."

Standing in front of the Joe Louis Fist Monument, Booker rang the alarm on his megaphone to get everyone's attention. When they looked his way. He gave a riveting, minute long speech that was getting ready to conclude.

We need to balance the scale, y'all. For real. You got, some students who are living house to house, couch to couch, shelter to shelter. And then you got some students who were born with a literal silver spoon in they mouth.

That ain't nobody's fault but y'all. Y'all brought them here. But I'm not here to point no fingers. I'm just here to Balance the Scale. If this is to be one nation under God, then we need to act like it; because right now the devil's agents and nonbelievers are working hard as hell... we need to balance the scale!

"That's right!" Manny shouted with his fist balled up after a heavy speech ended lightly.

Booker walked off with a different swagger about him. "B GARV, POTUS 2024... out!" He signed off, folding the megaphone.

After hearing his story and promises, the crowd was all in, "We need to balance the scale!" One man shouted, with his hands up in the air.

The crowd erupted as he concluded. Hope covered the motor city like the hood of a 1996 Chevrolet Monte Carlo. The city possessed two number one picks when they were only expecting one.

As the games, activities, and announcements ended, it was time for the draft to commence. "With the first pick, in the 2024 NFL Draft, the Chicago Bears select, Caleb Williams, quarterback Southern California," the Commissioner said, officially starting the Draft.

"Boo!"

"Boooo!"

Booker, Manny, and countless Lions fans booed for their rival's new selection at quarterback.

"Can't wait!" One man shouted, wearing a Honolulu blue Hutchinson jersey.

"Hutch is gonna fuck him up!" Another fan next to him in a black Hutchinson jersey shouted.

The section cheered so loud it caught the cameraman's attention. As he pointed his lens towards them, the crowd went berserk.

"With the second pick..." the Commissioner continued calling out name after name as college players shook hands with the Commissioner. One even picked him up.

Fifteen minutes started winding down on the large OLED screen located on stage. It displayed the home team's Honolulu blue and silver color scheme. Hometown fans at Campus Martius exploded with applause anxious for the update.

"We need a playmaker or a ballhawk on D," Booker said.

"Yessir! Somebody who can make an impact day one like B Branch did last year."

"Young bull started the season with a pick six!" Booker exclaimed. "You know how I feel about them Bama Boyz! They make great pros."

A Michigan girls flag football player and featured guest speaker announced the home team's first round pick. "The Dallas Cowboys have traded the 24th pick to the Detroit Lions. With the 24th pick in the 2024 NFL Draft, The Detroit Lions select... Terrion Arnold, Defensive Back, Alabama."

"Let's gooo!" Booker shouted.

Booker, Manny, and the fans all around them clapped, cheered, and slapped hands with anyone in sight until their palms reddened.

Afterwards, they cheered and jeered all night until the Commissioner wished them farewell. "That closes the first round. Thank you, Detroit, for a record setting night. Don't forget over the next two days, you can break the all-time NFL Draft record. Thank you, see you at seven o'clock tomorrow night." He reminded them over the loudspeakers.

"I think Brutha Holmes strikes again." Manny reflected, reading a draft profile folder being handed to him by an event worker.

"Mannn, duke knows how to pick em. If this wasn't an offensive draft, TA probably would've gone top five. Top ten fasho."

"One more dawg on D and we're Superbowl bound." Manny clapped his hands.

"Yessir!" Booker removed his phone from his pocket and opened his Ride Share app.

"You lucky you stay Downtown, man. Across the street like a muh fucka. I'll be stuck in traffic until midnight."

"You can take the guest bedroom if you need it. That's what it's for. Draft Day festivities starts at noon."

"I think I'm going to take you up on that offer, bro."

After Draft Night 2024, the state of Michigan had heightened expectations for multiple reasons. The sky was the limit. A record was set for fans in attendance during the Draft in Detroit. More than 750,000 people were present over the weekend. With over a quarter million of them being there on that particular day.

VI: On the Road

After a successful trip back home, Booker couldn't stop smiling. His campaign announcement was making a buzz over the weekend. During the ride home, his phone's notifications wouldn't stop interrupting his podcasts.

"Mama, there goes that man!" He shouted with one of the cohosts before his phone vibrated again and again… and again. Passing through Battle Creek on I-94W, Booker was twenty-five minutes from his condo after ninety minutes on the road.

Taking Exit 81, Booker took a trip to Woods Lake on the southwest side of town. The water was calling his name and he heard it loud and clear. Pulling into the entrance, Booker parked and walked downhill using stairs that had a steep slope. Kicking rocks and sticks along the way, he reached the parking lot and a gazebo that was located just off the shoreline.

Children played in the water and on land. Families barbecued and Booker was oblivious to it all. He sat, smiling from ear to ear, reading text messages and social media posts. Listening to voicemails and voice memos. Laughing aloud periodically, he was having the time of his life when he was interrupted by an older lady with peaked curiosity.

"Balance the scale!" She shouted, pumping her fists as attention crept their way.

Realizing who he was, an older man came over with a little boy. "We need to balance the scale!" He yelled. "Helluva speech, man. Helluva speech. Earmuffs, Junior." The man said to the boy.

"I felt every word. Especially the last line about the nonbelievers working hard. Someone stole three Cutlass Supremes from in front of my house in three different decades.

"Damn!" Booker jerked backwards. "Sorry, lil dude." He told Junior. "Earmuffs," he said. "Same thing happened to my Dad. The exact same thing. Same car, three times and everything."

"I see why Junior needed earmuffs. What are the odds?"

"Slim to none. Are you from here?"

"No, we're from all over. But that happened in Detroit. We moved here for the Promise when Junior started school."

"Detroit. That sounds more like it... unfortunately. That's wild, it happened in the same city too."

"Don't I know it. We just wanted to say hello. Can we get pictures with the next President of the United States?"

"Yessir!" Booker saluted the man. "And I get to get a picture with one of the next presidents too. Right, Junior?" Booker tugged on the boy's arm like an uncle.

"Yup! I wanna be a doctor, lawyer, football player, and the President of the United States. Just like you!"

"Not yet, lil dude." They laughed. "But soon. Y'all take care, now. I need to get some food." Booker waved, walking towards the stairs.

"What kind of man would I be if I didn't invite you to the barbeque?!" The man shouted, pointing to a group of people gathered by the lake. "Come on, Mr. Future President. We won't take *no* for an answer."

"Welp, like I always say in situations like this... lettuce!" Booker shouted, rubbing his hands together.

"Hey y'all, look what the wind blew in!" The man hollered.

Most of the crowd looked confused. While a small group of three couldn't wait to be introduced so they did so themselves.

"Hey Mr. President?" One lady shook his hand.

"Not yet ma'am." He chuckled. Experiencing déjà vu, he asked the woman, "Have we met?"

"I don't think so." She giggled. "Where you from? You look like a Detroiter."

"Highland Park. But close! I lived in Brightmoor for a little while when I was nineteen."

"Both of those are the same thing. Just say you're from Detroit and moved somewhere else in Detroit."

"Naw, we're our own city. We just share zip and area codes. Kind of like it's both of ours. We just keep our locations separate," he said, light heartedly as they walked away towards the food line.

"Yeah, OK. Long way from home, aren't you?"

"Home is definitely where the heart is. But right now, I'm with you and it feels like home."

"That was a good one, Mr. President." The lady blushed. Glancing down at her painted white tipped toenails, she looked back at Booker as the wind blew.

Softly, she asked, "B Garv…?"

"Booker Garvey III." He chuckled. "I don't usually give last names and suffixes on the first date. Since I skipped steps making it to the barbecue so soon. Why not?" He smiled.

"Date?" She asked. "You just met me."

"That didn't work?"

"No." She giggled. "Not this time."

"Well, I guess when I pick you up for one, it'll seem more date'y." He shrugged.

"Date'y?" She blushed again, laughing. "What does that even mean?"

"You know what it means." He joked. "Here, save your number in my phone." Booker handed it over. "I'll let you know where I know you from later on when it hits me."

"OK, President Garvey." She was still smiling then took his phone to save her number. The Sun kissed her dark brown, dimpled cheeks the way Booker wanted to.

Everyone watched the two, walk towards the grill as they made acquaintances with one another. "It smells *good!* around here," Booker said.

Grabbing a couple plates from the wooden table. It was covered with a blue and white checkered patterned tablecloth. He handed one of the plates to the woman, asking, "How can I call you if I didn't see what you saved it as? Unless it's something obvious like, *My Future Woman*."

"Funny, Mr. President." She giggled. "I guess you will need that information, huh? I'm Kenya."

"Like the country?"

"Yes, actually. Like the country."

"A woman of culture. Good to know." Booker smiled, licking his bottom lip.

"I was named for the country. I'm not from the country," she replied.

"Touché."

"I'm joking, President Garvey." She giggled. "My parents and I are actually from Kenya. I moved to America when I was a lil girl. We started out in Traverse City. But we've moved around a lot since then."

"How'd you get to Kalamazoo? You're a little too old for the Promise."

"You are so funny." She giggled.

"My Dad is an Engineer. He moved here after he was recruited by Grove Air and Automotives. I was still here from Western and my baby brother was getting ready to start school."

"Yo daddy work for GAA? I heard they get free flights and cars for the family," he queried.

"Something like that." She laughed.

"So, you went to Western too? What years?"

"Summer 2005 and I graduated Fall '07."

"You got out of there *quick!*" He snapped his fingers, fascinated by her accomplishment.

"I was dual enrolled during my senior year." She snickered.

"Oh, OK. Lil genius." He smiled. "I graduated in 2005 too. From high school at least but it took me a little longer to get out of Ol Western." He chuckled.

"I transferred there in Fall '07. We fasho missed each other because we already know most women stop going out *quick*." He snapped again. "Anywhere between second semester and sophomore year."

"Partying gets old kinda fast, don't you think?" She asked.

"That's probably what took me so long. I partied until my senior year… both of them."

"Both?"

"Three come to think of it." Booker slapped his forehead.

"Three!?" She laughed, covering her mouth.

"In my defense I switched majors when I got to Western. I used to say back then that I was a freshman with Junior credits." He chuckled, clearing things up.

"OK, that actually makes sense. What did you switch to and from?"

"I started in Business Management. I wanted to own a chain of convenience stores all over the country. I was going to open them across the street from middle schools and high schools."

"Aww." Kenya melted. "Ambitious."

"Then I got to high school and saw people snatching full candy bar boxes out of gas stations on our walk home. I'm talking a box of at least fifty. Dawg started passing them out up the street like he was Robin Hood or some shit."

Kenya laughed as he continued. "I switched to Elementary Education to try and save those kinds of people."

"Awww," she said, again. Slowly tearing up, she said, "I forgot you were a teacher. So that really was you up there? Your genuine self?" She asked, rhetorically. Touching his arm, she slowly rocked back and forth, shaking her head.

"What you going through over there?"

"The Garvey Effect, I guess. Is this what your date'y self does to every woman you meet? Woo us and live to woo another day."

Booker laughed, realizing she used a line from the same movie he quoted earlier. "That's probably where I know you from. Getting shot down at Homecoming '07." He pondered.

"I wouldn't have shot you down, but my Daddy might've. He shot down both of my college boyfriends." She admitted.

"Ohhh, so you're a daddy's girl?"

"Very much so and he's a big girl dad. I'm surprised he brought you this close to me and not over there with my uncles." She nodded to the table of men playing cards.

"That was your Dad?"

"Yup and my baby brother. I don't think he brought you over to ask me out on a date though. He was just being hospitable. Getting comfortable pretty quick there." She shook her head. "Asking if that's my Daddy and all."

"Why not?"

"Because you seem like the type to talk to women when you have a girlfriend."

"And what's the type?"

"Handsome with things going for himself."

"Thanks sweetheart. I admire you as well. I came over for a burger and some baked beans and I haven't gotten any yet! See what you do to me? Got me skipping meals to talk to you." He flirted, stepping out of line to finish the conversation.

"I do have a woman I'm seeing, but we're still dating. It's been a little over a year now."

"So why are you talking to me about dates? I just wanted to meet the president."

"Because a woman as put together as you *can't* be single. But I had to find out for myself once we started talking."

"Why not? I could be crazy."

"Very true." Booker chuckled, agreeing.

Kenya laughed, slapping Booker's arm. "I'm not crazy."

"That's what they all say." He laughed. "Right before doing something crazy."

"I'm not *they*..." Breaking up her sentences, she continued. "*I'm*... Kenya." She spoke slowly, softly, and flirtatiously.

"I see and that's why I'm talking to you as a dating man. It was lovvve at first sight." Booker sang a line from a hit song in the early 2000s.

"Whoa... Who's the crazy one now? *Mr. Love At First Sight.* You know, there's a show for people like you."

"I'm kinda joking." Booker laughed. "I will say, something made me look towards you when I caught you staring at me. All of this feels so right."

"Is that so? And staring? I wouldn't call it staring, I was trying to see who my Daddy and baby brother were talking to." She laughed, dismissing his claim. "You talk about me, but you're the celebrity who looked familiar. My Dad sent your speech to the family group chat at seven this morning."

"I'm just Booker." He chuckled.

"You're *her* Booker." Kenya corrected him.

"I thought you forgot?"

"Not that quick. How would she feel about us talking right now?"

"I told her I wasn't ready for a relationship for a reason."

"Well, you're not ready for me either then, Mr. President because I'm not date'y. You're either with me or you're not. How about you call me when you *are* ready for a relationship. An honest Politician is rare. I'm surprised you told the truth."

"I wouldn't lie to you, Kenya," Booker said.

"Remember that."

"I'm gonna remember it, write it down, take a picture…"

Kenya laughed hearing another line from one of her favorite movies. "I'm glad you like Friday. We might have a lot in common. Maybe I'll hear from you one day when you're not so… date'y."

"*When* you hear from me, it's for real." He motioned for her to get back in line ahead of him.

"Thank you." She smiled. "Please, don't waste my time."

Booker and Kenya fixed their plates with hamburgers, chicken wings, hot dogs, baked beans, potato salad, and all the other fixings. Making their way to the gazebo, Kenya's father motioned the two over to an empty table by him.

"I'm glad you met my daughter. She needs a good man like you," the man said.

"He's date'y, Daddy."

"Date'y, what is that?" He asked before guessing. "He likes to date?"

"Yup, he's dating."

"What man isn't date'y? At least he was honest. Most men would let you find out on your own. He told you the first day you met him."

Booker locked eyes with Kenya, smiling with a boyish, *I told you so* type of grin. "I had three wives when I met your mother and she had no desire to be the fourth." The man shrugged.

"We all change for the right woman, is the point."

He patted Booker on the back with a strong, heavy hand. "I'll let you two finish eating and getting to know each other. Nice meeting you, Mr. Future President. Hopefully, I'll be seeing you soon." The man shook Booker's hand and walked away towards the lake.

VII: Get Back to Work

Waking up around 8:15am, Booker slowly crawled out of bed to get ready to teach fifty-eight students in less than thirty minutes. Opening the dresser, he grabbed a navy blue Polo T-shirt and matching polo style shirt. Reaching for a pair of jet-black Levi 505 jeans, he pulled them up over his boxer briefs.

On the top shelf of his walk-in closet, he took a pair of Nike Air Penny 1 All Star Game basketball shoes. A blue G Shock watch and gold rope chain completed his look for the day. On the way to the door, Booker removed a chilled gallon of Ice Mountain spring water from the refrigerator. *Phone, Keys, Wallet,* he said to himself as he remote started his truck, locking the door behind him.

An elevator ride brought him to the lobby. Walking out the front door, he unlocked his truck as he approached it. Booker made his twenty-minute trip across town, mellowing the mood.

"Smoooooth operator. Smooth Operator…" Booker sang along, approaching a yellow light. Slowing to a halt, he shouted, "Now that's what I call theme music!" Smacking the window ledge of the driver's side door. Looking to his left, he saw a woman who had seen it all and was having a ball recording it.

"Oh you think it's funny? Then you don't know me, money… But you can." Booker licked his lips.

Honk! The drivers behind them blared at the now green light. "313-333-55—" The woman pulled off with all the horns blaring behind them. She drove away, failing to capture the remaining digits of his phone number. "55!" He shouted. "Damn! Y'all hating asses coulda waited!" Booker drove off slowly down the busy street, returning the favor.

"She was *cold,*" Booker shook his body, mad at himself for not being more aware. Cars honked their horns as they drove around him. Booker was driving abnormally slow out of spite.

POTUS 2024: BALANCE THE SCALE

    Finishing his route to the school, Booker walked the track behind the building and entered through the rear exit. He opened the classroom door, propping it open with a door stop. After writing math problems on the whiteboard for morning work, Booker walked over to the counter. Opening a cooler left for him by the morning cafeteria staff, he set up breakfast. Then left quarter sheets of paper next to it for the day's morning work.

    Students filed into the room, taking quarter sheets of paper from the counter against the wall. Booker was changing the date on the whiteboard as they entered. The morning was as uneventful as Booker's weekend was impactful on the opposite side of the state.

    Going through the morning routine teaching Math to two classes, Booker began to feel small and caged like a domesticated bird. Lunch time rolled around while Booker's pocket continued to vibrate as if it were his birthday. One of his group chats resurfaced to the top of his messages. It was his high school group chat who had finally caught wind of what happened over the weekend.

    Unaware, Booker began his lunch break as he walked out the side door of his classroom. Reaching into his pocket, he removed his keys to remote start his truck. Climbing in, he grabbed his phone, searching for one of his playlists.

    Seeing his home screen, he laughed reading the message previews. Marshall started it all, posting a link of the video that came his way. Having read all his texts, Booker replied.

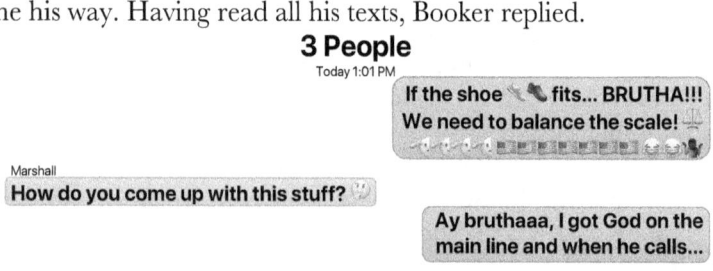

> **Yass better answer QUICK** 🔥
> **Before he calls somebody else!**
>
> Marshall
> **Yo ancestors would be so proud of you!** 😂😂😂
>
> **Aight, ion wanna hear shit about coming to the White House when I get in that mf** 📸
>
> Brock
> **I'm in there like a fetus. You tryna meet Up in Chicago. ORD to DCA @Marshall?**
>
> Marshall
> **Oh fasho!** 😏
>
> **Let's get it then!** 🤞
> Delivered

Booker's thumbs tapped off the screen with advice, jokes, and a confident prediction. He typed his last message, tapping the blue arrow to send the text. Ending his lunch break, Booker put his phone in the cupholder and listened to one of his workout playlists.

The slow day may not have been what the doctor prescribed for his inspirational needs, but it motivated him internally. After dropping off his students to the bus line after school, Booker conversed with his old teaching partner who moved to third grade.

"You see the draft? Terrion Arnold. We got another one of the Bama Boyz." Booker said.

"Yeah, I saw. Brad Holmes is making moves."

"Mannn." Booker agreed. "*When* he wins a ring in Detroit, it'll be worth ten like Big Mike on The Wood getting Alicia's number."

They laughed with students walking in every direction, headed to different destinations. Booker and Mr. Yandy recapped the draft until one little boy wearing a Spiderman shirt ran up to say, "Bye, Mr. Yandy." Then fist bumped him.

"See you tomorrow, Knox." Pounding fists, Mr. Yandy said, "Make sure you bring back my Spiderman shirt tomorrow."

Playfully tugging on the sleeve of the boy's shirt, he laughed and walked towards his bus.

"Ay, I saw your video about balancing the scale." Mr. Yandy was highly engaged.

"You did!?" Booker asked with excitement. "Where'd you see it? I didn't think it made it to this side of the state."

"It played after some of the draft coverage I was watching. Somebody posted it on YouTube. I was closing the app and saw you yelling in a megaphone." Mr. Yandy laughed out loud, hysterically.

Laughing along, Booker said, "We need to balance the scale." He motioned with his palms, pretending to be a balancing scale.

"How'd you get up there? I've never been that close to the Joe Louis Monument. I thought it was closed off."

"Hey, where there's a will, there's a way." He laughed again.

"Amen!"

"Naw, I'm boosting. It's just like crossing the street. The people around me were talking about some homeless people and how the city could've put them up with so much foot traffic that week. I was yelling in my megaphone starting chants all day on Draft Day, so I had a lil following." He chuckled.

"Then after hearing them talk, I went in my bag and pulled out the megaphone. My boy who I was with didn't know what was going on." Booker laughed, recalling the events leading up to his big moment. "I just happened to be in front of Joe Louis' fist when it all went down. That was pure luck of the draw."

"That's what's up." Mr. Yandy nodded his head.

"Appreciate it," Booker said. "Alright Yandy, I'm out of here. I gotta get something to eat. I missed lunch because I had detention." Pounding fists, he said, "The sacrifices we make."

"Every day."

Walking to the parking lot, Booker waved to Ms. Keaton and Mrs. Mabelle the 4th grade teachers from across the hall before remote starting his truck.

VIII: My Type of Lady

Besides smaller cities like his hometown Highland Park and Hamtramck. Small pockets of Detroit's Northend, East, and West sides of the city. Booker didn't have much motion or momentum at all. But things were certainly picking up steam in the political race.

Laughter from the living room was on repeat every five to ten minutes. "This mutha fucka is goofy!" Booker laughed. Picking up his phone, he texted a couple lady friends and a few of his group chats to see if they were following along.

Cycling through the names in his phone, he stopped for one he hadn't seen in some time. Opting to call versus text, he tapped the name in his phone, then it started ringing.

"Hello?"

"Hello, can I speak to Kenya?"

"It's me."

"What's up, Sweetheart?"

"Oh, Lord. Who did I give my number to this time? Who is this?" She asked, short on patience.

"Booker."

"Who?"

"Booker Garvey III? Balance the Scale?"

"Ohhhhhh."

———

"Hello? Hello? Hello!? Damn!" He shouted, flipping his phone to the couch.

Booker continued watching President Biden and President Trump go back and forth until he could take no more.

I really don't know what he said at the end of the sentence. I don't think he knows what he said either. Look... the TV continued until it didn't.

Booker's eyes bulged before he busted out laughing. "Enough, silence." Waving his hands, "I can't take this shit no mo," he said, aloud.

Booker turned his TV off. Instead, he researched topics to add to the live book *POTUS 2024* that he was writing. That's when he came across news articles from a month earlier.

Former President Donald Trump Found Guilty of Thirty-Four Felonies, he read.

"How Sway!?" Booker shouted as his phone rang. "Hello?" He answered. Not knowing what to expect.

"I thought you had a sense of humor, Mr. President?"

"You hung up on me!" He chuckled, gingerly. "That shit wasn't funny."

"I thought it was funny." She laughed, lightly.

"I see. How you been?"

"I'm OK."

"What's that mean?" Booker asked, hoping she would elaborate.

"It hurt a little when I deleted your number. That doesn't usually happen."

"Whoaaa!" Booker laughed. "It's like that? I thought you answered like that because you were mad at me."

"No. I had no clue who you were, and I was just in the city last week. I give my number out more than my name."

"What?" Booker continued laughing in disbelief.

"Seriously. I'd rather just give it to people and block them when they call or text, then to get called out my name for not. One guy called me after I gave him a fake number. Someone answered then he called me a bitch." She pouted.

"That's wild. I'm sorry you had to go through that, Lady. I saw something like that happen before with my own eyes. I was nineteen working at Lands' End and Sears at Oakland Mall. I'm at the A&W on lunch, minding my own bitness! Cutting up my chili cheese dog and I see a group of guys walk by some girls across the way. Dawg said something to whoever he was feeling.

"He must've gotten curved because he goes, *Well fuck you then!* I heard about that kind of shit happening, but I didn't believe it until I saw it." He empathized. "Y'all shouldn't have to go through that. Come correct or get some game. But take that L in peace, Playboy."

"OKKK." She laughed.

"You watch the debate tonight?" He asked jumping subjects for fresh conversation.

"Unfortunately."

"Biden needs to go ahead and get some white shoes and hit the beach. Let your toes hit the sand, man. It's time to retire." Booker joked.

"Not some white shoes though." She laughed. "You should've been up there tonight. I'd rather give you my vote than them."

"Ayyyeee, thanks, Lady." Booker smiled.

"If you're still running. You still want to be president when you grow up?" Kenya asked.

Pulling the phone away from his mouth, Booker shouted, "Yeah, but they won't let me! I get more support as an author than a Politician any day."

"Really?"

"Really. With a book, the cover is a big part of it. The person holding it is the other part. Once you talk to them it's a fifty-fifty chance they'll walk away with your book. With politics," Booker paused to call Kenya on FaceTime.

"Uhn uhn I hope you don't think I'm about to answer your FaceTime, do you?" Kenya asked.

"Ahhh dayyyuuummm," Booker pleaded, hoping to see her however he could get it. "I gotta use facial expressions to tell this story." Booker informed her.

"Welp, send a picture." She laughed, putting his hopes to rest.

"Alright, you too." Looking through his album, Booker sent her pictures with the best lighting and angles possible.

"You are not slick, Booker Garvey the Thirrrd." She spoke softly, while searching through her phone.

Kenya sent a few pictures of her at different events, wearing different types of attire. The first thing Booker said was, "Got... damn! I forgot how cold you were. Kenya, Kenya, Kenya." Booker admired her, cycling through the pictures over and over again.

"Don't Kenya, Kenya, Kenya, me." She blushed through the phone. "I met you two months ago and I'm just now hearing from you. I actually just deleted your number a couple weeks ago. I usually do it right away but I was hoping you'd call or at least text."

"I know but I'm running for president. I'm always somewhere." He chuckled again. "But next time we talk, it will be way less than two months from now."

"OK, Mr. President. Did you send your picture that goes with the story yet? Because what you sent is you looking at the Sun."

"What you mean? That's my model look." He laughed. "It's my serious face. But let me go ahead and do that reht nah!" He shouted into the receiver. Posing passionately, pointing ahead, he took a picture of himself.

Giggling on arrival, Kenya asked, "What are you doing?"

"That's how I am when I'm being all political n'shit." He chuckled as she laughed louder. "I could be in the middle of the best speech I ever gave." He paused. "Nothing!"

"Nothing?" She wondered, still laughing.

"Nothing! Not a clap, head nod, fist pump. Shit, most of the time people don't even look at you. It's a skill to avoid eye contact. They'll walk right past me and that loud ass megaphone like I'm invisible or some shit."

Booker was on a roll. Kenya couldn't stop laughing. "Stop, stop. Booker, just stop talking for a minute. I can't breathe. You are hilarious."

"I be saying some good stuff, Kenya. I don't mean to toot my own horn but *Ahhnnnn!*" He mimicked a semi-truck's horn.

"I wrote this one speech about haves and have-nots. I said we'd rehabilitate nonviolent felons who made millions to tap into their minds. You would've thought I said pardon everybody. One old lady tried to take my megaphone. Talking about, *I oughta be ashamed of myself.*"

"You are so funny!"

"I'm just saying. Forty-Five caught thirty-four felonies. I just found out it was over hush money for a porno star." Booker shook his head. "I thought it had something to do with espionage the way the media machines gassed it.

"This man was allegedly knock'n boots and tried to get away with it. That sounds like an alleged problem between him, his wife and that man's family. Not a bill for taxpayers."

"Alright, Mr. President!" Kenya clapped her hands, nodded her head, and secured her AirPods as Booker continued.

"It's smooth though. It's only June," he said, confidently.

"Exactly. You still have five months. A lot can happen in five months."

"My type of lady."

"Mmmm Hmm. Two whole months later."

Booker and Kenya conversed all night until the early morning. "I don't want to hang up because two months is a long time to go without talking to you again but I'm sleepy, Mr. President and you have school in the morning."

"I do. But I'll be up for a couple more hours. I have some writing to do. As a teacher slash author, I work when people sleep. Nap when they're getting ready for work and work when they work."

"Why do you still teach? I don't know many teachers with new trucks and hilltop condos."

"It's not *that* new and the hill is not *that* high," he said, humbly.

"Booker, please. I can see it from my office."

"For real?"

"Yah."

"Oh…"

"Don't they shoot the fireworks off there at the lake?"

"Something like that." He chuckled.

"That's why I asked. Doesn't seem like you need to."

"I just started writing a speech on teacher pay. Long story short… somebody had to go through it to let you know what's going on." He shrugged as if she could see him.

"Alright, Mr. President!" She shouted.

IX: World War Willis

Over the next couple months, things moved in slow motion. Not because of effort but results. Booker did well campaigning in neighboring cities because of his book trail as an author. But he was failing to make up ground on a national level. He built relationships with citizens and local businesses in smaller cities like Vicksburg but not much farther.

Cruising down the street in his 2020 Chevrolet Tahoe, Booker was riding high with just his thoughts. Merging onto US-131 South, Booker said, "Get directions to Sunset Lake. Vicksburg, Michigan," into the receiver as it recited the directions over the stereo system. "Continue for seven point three miles." The GPS instructed while Booker sped south.

"Arrived." sounded through the speakers as Booker reached his destination. Booker eased into the parking lot entrance, admiring a stunning view of the Sun dancing on Sunset Lake. Turning left, he parked his truck. Getting out, he grabbed his megaphone and approached the first group of people he saw.

"Hey," an older man said from his seat. He waved him over. "You look like you have something to say," the old man said, slowly and seriously. As long as it took him to complete his sentence, Booker knew it had to be important. The man was very stern with his words although they lacked energy.

He signaled Booker over to him again but quicker. He whispered his words the best he could, shaking his head left to right first. Booker approached the old man to see what he wanted.

The man pointed to the fishing lines that were posted against the rail ahead of them, belonging to the fishermen nearby. Then the old man pointed to Booker's megaphone, saying, "You'll alert the fish." He continued shaking his head, no.

Booker replied, "Ohhh." Quietly shaking his head in agreement, he walked back to his truck. Booker traded his megaphone for a roll of QR stickers, autographed photos, campaign posters, and a lawn sign. Planting the lawn sign on a strip of grass by the entrance, he walked over to the old man, gave him a poster, a QR coded sticker and asked, "When's the last time you saw the president fish with the people?" The old man smirked.

"I'm the wrong person to ask." The old man smiled big and wide. "Jerry Ford and I played on the gridiron together from 1900 and 32 to 1900 and 34. Won two championships together and you know what we would do every summer before the season?"

Booker was all ears knowing a firsthand account of pure American history was headed his way. "I'm going to guess you went fishing?"

"Fishing." The old man confirmed. "Jerry was one of a kind. He stood up with your people too. Way before he was president. You ever heard of Willis Ward?" The old man asked, covering his cough as he gasped for air between breaths.

Booker gave the man his water while he regained his composure. "I haven't. Was he a Politician?"

"Willis was a lot of things. He was involved in politics, but I wouldn't say he was a Politician. Willis was the best athlete I ever did see. Ran like a gazelle, jumped like a bunny rabbit, strong as an ox, and smart as a whip!" The old man was having a burst of energy mid flashback.

"Willis Ward was a track star and whoever was on the other side of him on the gridiron was in for a battle all game long. World War Willis Ward." Another spell of coughs interrupted his speech.

Soon after, a middle-aged woman with salt and pepper hair rushed to check on him. Her gym shoes matched her hair and outfit in color. "Daddy, are you OK?"

"I'm fine," he said. The old man shooed her before she reached his side. "Don't you see grownups talking!?" He shouted, taking several small sips of water.

The woman looked confused and stood still for a moment before being shooed away again. "Willis ended up in Law. He was a Lawyer and a Judge." The old man leaned back in his seat, crossed his fingers across his stomach and continued the story. "Makes sense why he did."

"Yeah? Why's that?" Booker asked.

"Life is a lot different now than it was then for your people," the old man said, loosely.

"Don't I know it. My grandparents were born in the 1910s and 1920s. I sat at their feet with opened ears plenty of nights growing up in the 1990s," Booker replied.

"You know what you can without being there. But I was there. Dark times. They were some dark times," the old man shook his head. His words were beginning to be spaced farther apart. "The Georgia Tech game, 1900 and 34… that was the beginning of the end. We were the champs! Back-to-back…" The old man clapped his hands in anguish.

Seconds later, his daughter began making her way over to the old man. Only to be shooed away once more before nearing him. "We lost a lot of big men on campus to graduation that year. Going into the Georgia Tech game… two games into the season," the old man paused. "We hadn't scored a point." He shook his head.

Booker laughed at the old man's sense of humor starting to show. "We didn't play like they do now. Pass, pass, pass, pass, pass… I'm open." The old man pumped his arm like he was throwing a football and catching it himself. "Michigan Men ran the football. Right at you, over, and through you. When they're tired and can't tackle any more, we kept on running."

Booker was all in and the old man was starting to gain momentum. "When we did throw the ball, it was to get ahead or to stay ahead. Football is a brute sport. Supposed to be. Mono e mono. Who's the toughest, meanest, strongest, son of a bitch on the gridiron that Saturday!

"Now… Everything is so finesse. Everyone wants to be a track star. Know what it looks like to me?" The old man asked, throwing Booker a bone.

"What's that?" He asked, chuckling.

"Ballet!" Everybody wants to run or dance away from contact. It's ONE WAY!" The old man shouted. "To the endzone, north and south! Depends on who has the ball. I'm not talking about being fast. It's all the wiggling." He clapped, then held his hands to shake his body. Doing a juke move.

"I hear you loud and clear!" Booker rejoiced, smiling. "I played linebacker, tight end, and a little wide receiver. So, I understand. It makes my job easier." Booker shrugged.

Booker was having the time of his life walking down memory lane with the old man. "You'd probably be one of us. You've got the discipline. I can tell by your physique. You didn't let me scare you off so you must be tough!" The old man spoke with low volume and high intensity. He was fired up.

"What I saw last Sunday... they not like us. Nothing like us at all. Saw one fella wearing 100k in jewelry they said. Another did something my great grands called the Grizzley."

"The Griddy."

"Eh?!" The old man said, "What's that?" Asking Booker to repeat it.

"It's called the Griddy." Booker laughed.

"In '32, they would've called it benched because that's where he would've ended up. We'd be benched if we did something like that. Maybe even kicked off the team altogether. My coach snatched somebody off the field once in '34. We stunk it up that year. He said he'd rather look bad with ten instead of looking bad for no reason with eleven."

Booker laughed hysterically.

"What?" The old man asked, wondering what was so funny.

"You're a funny man, sir."

"Hue is fine."

"Nice meeting you, Mr. Hue. I'm Booker."

"Booker?"

"Yes, Sir?"

"Don't ever call me Sir or Mr. I said, Hue!" The old man said with precise intentions.

"Alright, Hue." Booker chuckled humbly in a mellow mood.

Booker and Hue talked about Michigan football for over an hour. Hue gave detailed accounts of the times, trials and tribulations players of his time faced. "The last two games of the '33 season weren't easy at all. We went scoreless in a game that snapped our sixteen-game win streak. Ended in a tie. Willis got a concussion that game. I know he did.

"He caught a twenty-one-yard pass, got tackled and his head hit the ground so hard, you heard it on the sidelines. In those days, your teammates picked you up. You shook it off and kept on playing. That's just what Willis did."

"Tough as nails." Booker nodded his head.

"Tough as nails. The next game, he caught a beautiful thirty-seven-yard touchdown. Caught it in stride like he was running track! He beat Jessie Owens in the sixty and the sixty-five-meter high hurdles too by the way. Willis was something else. That was our second year getting crowned champions of the gridiron."

"That sounds like a movie. What happened to him? Did he get hurt? How come we don't hear about him like Jessie Owens?" Booker was invested in Hue's story like a full-time broker.

"Well… we weren't that good our senior year. Lost all but one game that season," Hue said. He was defeated and losing energy.

"The game we won. We won it for Willis. Georgia Tech said they wouldn't play us if he played. He was the only Afro American on our team for a long time. Was the first in forty years. First since George Jewett did it in the late 1800s."

Booker hadn't learned so much in one sitting since his undergraduate studies. "Campus had already changed once booze was legalized and folks started partying on game days. Campus was becoming a lot more outspoken. Petitions went around for folks in support of letting Willis play. Fifteen hundred people signed, and it still didn't matter. Bonfires… didn't matter.

"They were starting to say they had to bench Willis for his safety after the death threats started coming in. Players for Georgia Tech started saying they'd hurt him. It got ugly, real ugly. Jerry Ford was going to sit out with him. His old man said it was a decision he had to make for himself. He only played because Willis told him he had to play for us, the team."

The Sun had repositioned itself during their conversation and was now directly over the two men, casting shadows on the ground. "We played and won. Then lost every game after it that season. Yeah, we lost a lot of seniors to graduation but I don't think we were ever the same after that Georgia Tech game.

"Willis wasn't that's for sure. He trained hard, Booker. Stayed in the weight room, chopped logs. The man pushed and pulled cars in the summertime."

"Damn," Booker said under his breath. *That's why I didn't go pro,* he thought.

"He told me with his own mouth it was getting hard to train, knowing he could get benched any game. Looked me right in the eyes and said, *What if we were winning like the last couple years and that was how they knocked us off the top of the hill.* I can still hear his voice in my head today from when he said it."

"You still see him?" Booker asked.

"At the cemetery. It's only two of us still kicking from those days. We talk every year after the Ohio State game. He lives in Florida now."

"You got a lot to talk about lately. Congrats being back on top."

"Yeah, it's about damn time," Hue said.

Shortly after, his daughter returned with two teenagers. They were carrying coolers with a tall, large man holding the family's fishing gear.

"Hey, Hue. You met a new friend?" The man asked, loading things into the flatbed of the family truck. Hue didn't respond, he just repositioned himself in the chair he sat in.

"Yeah, they've been talking for hours now." Hue's daughter had nervous laughter during their introduction. "Hi." She extended her hand towards Booker. "Karen," she said.

"Hi, Booker. Nice meeting you." He shook her hand.

"Todd." The man added his hand to the meet and greet.

"Booker." He nodded, shaking hands.

"I didn't know Grandpa could talk?" One of the boys said as the other quickly elbowed him.

"Are these your sons?" Booker asked in small talk.

"Yeah. This is Clay and that's Herm." Todd put his hands on the boy's backs as they shook hands.

"You two play football like your Granddad?" Booker asked.

"Grandpa played football?" Herm asked aloud.

"I didn't know that either." Todd whispered behind his hand. Karen nudged him as he exposed family business.

"Nice meeting you, Booker," Karen said. She shook his hand again as they helped Hue from his seat.

"God's speed." Hue shook Booker's hand as they walked him to the car. The man's hands were round at the knuckles, callus on the inside, and cold in temperature.

"Pleasure was mine, Hue." Booker saluted the old man as he got into Karen's sedan, while the boys rode in the truck with Todd. "The pleasure was mine." He repeated, waving as they departed.

Electing against leaving so soon himself, Booker sat in his truck for a while. Recording voice memos and jotting down notes in a brown leather journal. "Call Manny." He instructed, pressing a button on his steering wheel.

"Forty-Seven, what's good?"

"What up dooooe?" Booker asked, stretching out the word.

"I still can't believe you're running for president, dawg. You really wasn't bullshit'n."

"When you ever known me to be a bullshitter!?"

"You definitely ain't a bullshitter. You's a silly, goofy, funny ass muh fucka. But you're not a bullshitter."

"My man!" Booker laughed, blown away, not knowing what to say. "Somebody gotta do it bro. Biden..." Booker paused. "Biden's doing the best he can do, man," Booker said from the driver's seat.

"Yeah, he needs to sit his ass down somewhere."

"Dawg," Booker said in short. "That's kind of why I hit you up. I was watching the debate a few weeks ago and if that's my competition, I'm about to go all in. Remember when I said, next time I call you, it's for real?"

"What's up? What you need, Book?"

"A Campaign Manager."

"Shit, alright. Yea... What I gotta do?"

"Damn if I know." Booker laughed. "I was using you like a Little Joker in Spades because you were a poli sci major. But I just remembered right damn now that you switched majors to Communications the same semester I switched to Education."

"Ay, I can do *something* till we figure it out. What you thinking?"

"Dawg, I just talked to this old ass man..." Booker stopped. "I try not to use the O-word, bro."

Manny laughed loudly as Booker removed the phone from his ear, checking its time stamp.

"For real." Booker chuckled. "I can only hope to be his age one day. He had to be a hun bun plus. I'ma say one o'seven because it sounds nice. If he was a college freshman at Michigan in 1931, he was born in 1913-ish.

"So, peep game. One of our elders n'shit right?" Booker said, safely. "Not an old man." Booker laughed. "An elder. He's one eleven-ish. You know what the I mean, shit."

"Fasho." Manny laughed. "I got you."

"Dawg played football for U of M and won a couple chips with President Gerald Ford."

"He's from the Ru," Manny added.

"I found that out Googling presidents from Michigan and Grand Rapids popped up not too long ago. I took a trip to his museum earlier this year. Then I ended up kick'n with his old teammate for two, three hours, a few minutes ago."

"That's wild."

"As a muh fucka," Booker said. Researching President Ford while on the call, he asked, "You ever been to the museum?"

"Yea, we used to take field trips there."

"That's dope. Y'all prolly left feeling like being president was possible."

"Naw, for real though. We did."

"I'm feeling motivated. Dawg was talking some real shit."

"Had to be, bro. You know how much has changed since he was born?"

"Celebrations, fasho." Booker laughed. "He said his coach woulda snatched a muh fucka off the field in real time if they hit the Griddy after a touchdown."

Booker and Manny bounced between subjects for a little while until Manny made his first announcement as a staff member. "Biden dropped out," he said in short. "Three hours ago."

"You bullshit'n!? Damn!" Booker flipped his phone to the passenger seat. Shaking his head, he picked up the phone saying, "My bad, bro. I just saw a big as L flash in front of my eyes, dawg."

"Yeah." Manny chuckled. "I see you know what that means."

"Kamala's coming."

"You know it."

"She's about to take *all* the voters I need, bro." Booker sobbed, dramatically, "Women!" He shouted, continuing to meltdown.

"Yeah, man. That's a strong possibility." Manny admitted. So, I've been researching positions, I'll be like a Consultant, slash Field Organizer. Or something like it.

"I'll let you know what muh fuckas say about you and keep my boots on the ground. Seeing what the people want *from* the president." He emphasized. "As far as being yo Campaign Manager; I'ma look for events to go to for publicity and any kind of speaking engagements I can find for you."

"My dawg, good look, bro. That kinda brought me back to reality, mane. I can't even lie. I legit thought I had a shot against Biden and Forty-Five.

"I know one muh fucka with enough money to throw at a campaign and not miss it. But I haven't talked to him since I met him. Dawg told me to hit him up when I figured out what I wanted to do with my life. That's the Big Joker. I was waiting until we started promo for the book to play the Big Joker since they crossover."

"I remember when you met him. We stayed at Southern Woods back then."

"Yup." Booker laughed. "I can't even hit him up no more. I gotta keep the Big Joker tucked again. Madam Vice President is taking *all* my votes, bro. I gotta sway Mom's and my sister now."

"Maybe." He chuckled. "She might be like Michelle Obama and doesn't want to be president."

Checking his email in the background screen of the conversation, Booker read an email. "Dawg."

"What's up?"

"It's official, I just got an email from Biden's campaign endorsing her presidential run."

"Ay…" Manny paused. "It is what it is. Better get on yo Journey shit and Don't Stop Believing!" Manny motivated.

"See what I'm saying. That's why you are what you are on this campaign staff, bruh!" Booker shouted. "If anybody asks, you're my Campaign Manager and we'll split the other jobs. Fuck it."

"Fuck it!" Manny confirmed.

X: Sabbatical

The colors of the leaves on the trees weren't the only changes being made during the fall season. Booker's outlook on the election was fading fast. Nothing he did seemed to draw any attention or notoriety, until it did.

Ring, went Booker's phone, vibrating next to him. He was sitting at the kitchen table, trying to figure out his next steps as a political figure. At the top of the list was a back-to-school rally for students in grades pre-K through 12th. It was a short list. Booker was running out of ideas.

"Hello?" He greeted, answering the phone.

"Book, what's good?" Manny asked.

"Not shit, brodie. Not shit in this political race at least. Dawg... not shit! I'm about to get waxed!" Booker admitted, already feeling defeated.

"You *were* about to get waxed. I got a plan."

"Well, talk to me Campaign Manager!"

"Kamala Harris—"

"Is stealing my voting base by the second!" He confessed, snapping his fingers. Finishing Manny's sentence for him.

"For now," Manny assured him. "Peep game, she's going to be in Grand Rapids this week. Friday at Riverside Park—"

"Riverside, mutha fucka!" Booker shouted, imitating a movie character.

"Aight, Bishop. Ol Juice watching ass." Manny joked. "I'm signing us up. We gotta study an experienced Politician. The way they talk and deliver speeches n'shit. I know she's the competition but she's still, muh fuck'n Madam Vice President!" Manny shouted into the receiver.

"Truuue!" Booker agreed. "Shiiit, lettuce!"

"Bet. You should be getting a text and email with details soon. We might have to hit the road bright and early. So don't do anything I wouldn't do Thursday night."

"You worried about me? On a Thursday night?" Booker laughed. "You should be. But I'll be ready whenever it is."

"Aight, bro. I was just trying to catch you before you had something on the floor for the weekend. It's already Wednesday."

"My dawg!"

"You know it. Bring the megaphone. Yo passionate ass needs to steal some votes."

"Who you telling? But that megaphone only works on Lions fans, dawg." Booker shook his head. "But I'll bring it anyway."

Booker hung up the phone feeling optimistic about the weekend. The last large crowd he spoke to in the state of Michigan kickstarted his political career. It wasn't the first time Booker took the independent route. He started his writing career the same way under a pseudonym before signing with a major publisher.

The drive to Grand Rapids didn't seem any different in terms of traffic volume. Early morning drivers made their way to work while Booker and Manny went back to school. "Alright, make a right up here," Manny guided, pointing to the street from the passenger seat.

"Damn, I didn't think it'd be this many people up here already. It's only…" Manny looked at the clock in standstill traffic, "8:34. Doors open at ten and it said not to arrive later than one."

"So, it'll probably start around what, three or four?"

"Probably so, yeah."

"Bet," Booker replied, nodding his head. "That's a clean six, seven hours of vote larceny, baybeeeh!" He calculated, shaking Manny's hand.

"Let's get it. How you gon do it? Just start talking on this muh fucka?" Manny asked, grabbing the megaphone from the backseat. He didn't know where to start himself.

"I don't know. That's my only problem," Booker deflected. "What you think?"

"Ay, start with a, *good morning*."

"My cuz say, *keep it simple*." Booker chuckled.

Turning down a residential street with not much traffic, Booker asked, "Think I'll get towed if we park here?"

"Maybe?"

"I ain't risking it. Not today! We'll be here all night trying to find a ride with all these people here." Booker circled the block, looking for parking spots closer to the park.

"What about up there?" Booker pointed at the grassland next to the entrance where cars had started parking.

"Probably not but today might be different."

"Right, they can't tow us all… I hope." Looking around him, Booker made a move. "This is the time to do it with everybody stuck at lights."

Booker drove forward before reversing up the curb and onto the grass of the park right next to a white SUV. Cars approaching the areas in both directions began to follow suit as they filled up the row within minutes. "Alright, we good-good. It's way too many of us here now."

Rolling down the window to see what the man next to him wanted, he had Booker's attention. "Good call parking up here. I didn't know where to park." He laughed, tipping his hat.

"Gotta think quick sometimes." Booker replied, chuckling with the man.

"See ya." He smirked, leaving with the woman he was with.

"How many waters you got back there?" Manny asked, wondering while the window went back up.

"Couple cases."

"Cool! Get some QR codes, stick them shits to the waters, small talk a little. Shake some hands, kiss some babies and we're good to go." Manny shrugged.

"That's a good idea. I'm wit it." Booker and Manny spent the next ten minutes peeling stickers and placing them on forty-eight, 16.9oz bottles of water. "That's the last one?" Manny asked.

Booker looked to see that he took the last bottle from the driver's side cupholder. "Yeah, that's it. We out."

Manny grabbed his jacket from the back seat and exited the truck. Booker's next stop was to his camera bag. He removed two Velcro straps that secured the company's Nikon cameras. Booker attached the lens with a stronger zoom to the 4K camera. Securing both cameras around his neck on both sides of his body, he reached in the back seat pocket. Then removed a few plastic store bags. Giving a some to Manny, Booker began filling his bags with water bottles.

Walking over to the long line of people, Booker and Manny looked at each other. Realizing things already hadn't gone the way they planned. "Bro, this line don't look shit like the crowds on TV bump'n Meg, Twerk'n, n'shit," Booker said.

"Dawg, everybody here is either retired or stepped out of the office. Not took off... Stepped out of the office." Manny joked. "New plan, we gotta find some AKA's you know they're around here somewhere. We gon have to D9 our way in first, bro."

"You know I love the AK-uhs, bruh," Booker shook Manny's hand. "Deltas, SGRho's, Zetas. All of them!" He smiled.

"I know you do." Laughing, Manny repeated, "I know you do. AKA's first. After that, the next group of women we see."

"Bet. There they go right there," Booker said, pointing to a group of middle-aged women in the first halves of their lives wearing pink and green colors throughout their wardrobe.

"Don't go over there reckless, bro." Manny advised. "They're career woman fasho."

"You know, ion give a fuck." Booker warned Manny of what may or may not happen.

"I know, that's why I said it, muh fucka." Booker and Manny shared a laugh before getting back to business.

"I code switch, G." Booker shrugged. "I'm Booker from HP for my *Ghetto Girls*." Booker sung an old tune. "And I'm Mr. Garvey, teacher turned author for the career women. Most of the time I'm a lil of both. But I love em all the same, you dig what I'm saying, mane?" Booker asked, shaking hands with Manny.

"Aight, aight. My bad. College was what? Twelve, thirteen years ago now? I haven't seen you in action with many career women. Except ol girl."

"Who?" Booker asked for a refresher.

"From down south." Manny tilted his head.

"Ohhh, so you dig what I'm saying!" Booker and Manny laughed as they approached the group of women.

"I can dig it. I underget it." Manny shook his head.

Stopping a few people ahead of the group they targeted, Booker began slowing down and breathing heavily. As he got closer, his hands were on his knees. Manny looked at him with confusion, not knowing what was going on. Reaching into the bag, he took a few sips of water before saying, "Y'all took my breath away." Booker smiled at the ladies, making eye contact with each of them as he handed them a water bottle.

"Aww," some said. While others laughed, joked, and jeered.

"Gon head and *Skee-Wee* your Soror on." He waved, walking to the back of the line with Manny.

"You a badd muh fucka, Book. I don't know *how* that shit worked. But it worked."

"Uhhn huh. We gon see em later too with all that pink and green. They gon scan that QR code too watch. It was about seven or eight of them."

"Cold too," Manny acknowledged.

"Mannn, the one with the brown hair, ooh wee, Skee-Wee." Booker moved dramatically, having movements with each word.

Walking to the back of a line that seemed to never end, they finally found a spot. "I'ma hit the bathroom real quick." Booker pointed to the Port-a-Potty as he handed Manny his megaphone.

Passing out QR code stickers there and back, Booker took the megaphone from Manny. "I just saw a dawg ass Sprinter. That muh fucka was blacked out with black rims, a big ass tinted window across the side of it, and black snow tires." Manny was blown away. Waving his arm left to right to demonstrate.

"Word?"

After almost an hour, the line wasn't getting any shorter and the doors hadn't opened yet. Booker looked at his wrist, "9:48," he read aloud. "I'm about to work the crowd for these next ten minutes, bro."

Stepping out of line, Booker powered on the megaphone and addressed the people of Grand Rapids. "Good morning!"

Good Morning! The group responded strongly. Manny smiled wide and proud at the crowd's liveliness, recording it all in 4k on his phone.

"I'm Booker Garvey III, if I could get everyone to take out your phones and go to the website www." He paused while the audience responded quickly and promptly.

"Is he working the event?" The woman behind Manny, asked.

"No, he's running for office. He's giving the website now." Manny nodded towards Booker.

POTUS 2024: BALANCE THE SCALE

"L-O-T-T-4-8-2-0-3 slash a-b-o-u-t. Make sure *about* is in lowercase letters." Booker's prompts received mixed reviews from the crowd. "That's www.LOTT48203.com/about." He spoke over their voices.

"It's just him... In a suit. Is this a rap tape or something?" One man asked, disappointed.

"I thought he worked here," a teenager said to his mother.

"Why does he have a megaphone? They're not going to let him take that in there, are they?" Another asked her friends.

Chatter began to drown out Booker's voice as he powered off his megaphone and got back in line. "I shoulda wore my jersey, bro. The Lions are 3-1 right now," Booker told Manny in defeat.

"It's good, Book," Manny said, pounding fists. Laughing at Booker's pain. "They thought you had updates. It's 10:00 and the doors just opened. That's all." Manny was still laughing. "Right place, wrong time."

Walking with the line one step at a time, Booker had to figure out how to get his confidence back. To his left, he saw vendors who set up shop, selling their products to people walking by. "Ay, let me get some of your waters." Booker nodded at Manny's bag.

"Aw shit, what you thinking?" Manny asked as the line came to another stop.

"I'm about to pass them out behind us. Then walk ahead and pass out QR stickers to see how many people drop them," he said before leaving. "I'll be right back."

Booker set off looking for women in groups of three or more. "Hey ladies." He waved. Your professor would respect you're playing hooky to see Madam Vice President and not because of a hangover." Booker approached one group, speaking quietly.

"You better stop, I have a daughter your age," one of the ladies said.

"Is she here?" Booker looked the woman up and down then looked around at the crowd, asking, "Where she at?"

"She will be, and I'll tell her..." The woman paused, waiting for Booker's name.

"Booker. Nice to meet you ma'am."

"There we go. Now, Booker. If you're going to be dating my daughter… I'll tell you now. She's a diva. Can you handle that?" The woman asked.

"Ma'am, with all due respect. The question is… can she handle me!?" Booker was fully animated, pointing at himself.

"Boy, if you don't give me a water and get out of here." The woman laughed with her friends as Booker gave them all bottles of water. "See y'all later." He waved, walking away. "We're here all day."

With his last four bottles, Booker walked over to what appeared to be four generations of the same direct blood line. The eldest of them rode by slowly with the group on a motorized scooter that was elevated to eye level, wearing a large purple headband and matching earrings. While the others looked to be in good physical shape. Presumably walkers due to their slim, athletic build and sportswear.

"VIP is on the other side of the park, ladies. You're in the wrong line. You all get to skip general admission." Booker said with admiration.

"Oh, you're such a sweetheart," the second eldest replied.

"Here you go." Booker handed each of them a water bottle with a smile. "You all from here?" He asked.

"Jenison," the second youngest said. "Thank you," she added, taking the water bottle. "I'm Joan, this is my mother Melissa and her mom, my grandmother, Sally and this is my daughter, Samantha," Joan said, introducing the family."

"Nice to meet you ladies. I'm Booker." He delicately shook their hands. "I thought you all were backup singers for the group and Madam Sally was singing lead. I'm sorry. I guess you'll have to wait in line with the rest of us. I apologize." Booker revealed a surprise with matching facial expressions as he walked towards the front of the line.

Standing on his toes, he was finally able to see the entrance. Holding his camera high above the crowd, he took a picture documenting the day.

POTUS 2024: BALANCE THE SCALE

 Making his way back towards Manny, he passed out all of his QR coded stickers. Then powered on his megaphone again. "LO-TT, 48-203!" Booker shouted in a cadence into the megaphone.
 Finding a hilled top, he walked up the side of it. With the Sun beaming on his back, he chanted. "LO-TT, 48-203! LO-TT, 48-203!" He continued, pumping his fist.
 For the first twenty seconds people laughed and pointed. Some joined in. Halfway through the minute, Booker was old news and was being asked, "Sir?"
 "Yes?" He responded, talking directly into the microphone.
 "I'm going to need you to take your megaphone back to your car," the man said.
 "My megaphone is not on the prohibited items list." Booker objected.
 The security guard seemed to be weighing his options while Booker continued. "If the people want me to put the megaphone down, then I will!" He shouted into the microphone.
 Shortly after, the line began to boo, loudly. Some whistled and pleaded. "Please get back in line, child. Before they drag you out of here." An older woman warned him, pointing with each word.
 Booker's jaw dropped and all he could do was laugh at himself. Folding its handle, he flipped the megaphone out of his hand. It rolled downhill, bouncing in the air on the uneven portions of land.
 Walking to the bottom, he found Manny on his way back to the line where he stood quietly, shaking his head. "Book, it's cool, bruh." Booker didn't respond. He just kept shaking his head. "Ay, if it makes you feel better, at least this isn't your event." Manny looked at the bright side to things.
 "Mannnn." Booker dismissed Manny once again, waving his hand in front of him, saying, "Pshhh."
 The next twenty minutes, Booker stood silently, wondering where things went wrong. "I thought this shit was gonna be easier than this, dawg," Booker said. The line was finally moving at a steady pace as they approached the entrance gate to the event.

Removing their belongings, they placed them in plastic bowls and slid them through the metal detector. "How are you doing, Sir?" An FBI agent asked. A younger man in his early thirties with a wavy Caesar.

"Good, you?" Booker replied.

"Good, thanks. Could you take the lens off of both cameras, please?" He asked.

Booker removed the lenses as the agent peeked inside. "Alright, thanks. Enjoy your day."

"Thanks. You too."

Entering the park, Booker spotted the food trucks right away. Manny did the same with the Port-a-Potty. "I'm about to grab something to eat," Booker said.

"I'm not really hungry. Here, grab me some street corn, a chicken taco with whatever comes on it, and a chicken tamale. I'll need it later once it gets packed. I'm sho." Manny reached into his wallet and removed a twenty.

"Keep it," Booker rejected. "Just pay for whatever we get after we leave. It's only twelve. We're here til at least five."

"Bet." Manny accepted as he walked to the line.

Getting in line, Booker was relieved to see it wasn't as long as he thought it would be with the door being open for two hours already. "Can I help you?" The woman asked.

"Can I get a loaded chicken nacho, four chicken tacos, two street corns and three chicken tamales," Booker ordered.

"$46.64," the woman said, waiting for payment.

Booker swiped his card asking, "How long do you think?"

"About twenty minutes." She answered, truthfully. "We're kind of backed up."

Damn, I should've asked that first. Booker thought to himself, waiting next to a large stack of water cases piled on top and next to each other. Leaning over the top of them, Booker pulled out his phone to YouTube until his name was called.

"Cam, Cam," his phone went as he was distracted by an open food container that was placed in front of him. Booker couldn't tell what was going until a brown skinned woman with cornrows, black framed glasses, a hoop nose ring, and glossed lips caught his eye. "Is that mine?" He asked.

"Nope, his." She pointed quickly, stepping backwards.

Booker looked closely to see that a bee had made its way to her lunch. "Lucky bee."

"Why?" She asked, trying to get back to her Mexican cuisine.

"Because it gets to eat lunch with you." He smiled at the woman as she laughed.

The woman continued to laugh, almost nonstop. It was at that moment, Booker realized he was taking another loss. "So that's what you've been telling everybody?" The woman asked him.

"What you mean?" Booker didn't have a clue what was going on and it was starting to show.

"You're the water boy, right?"

"Water boy?" Booker laughed hysterically. Almost the same as the woman moments earlier. "I can't be the water man at least? Water wuh-water man," Booker rapped in a familiar rhythm.

"OK, fine. But you skipped me and my girl a few times. Water *man*. So, you're not that good at it. Especially not good enough to be bragging and remixing songs."

"My bad." Booker leaned his head back and chuckled. "We were looking for groups. Here you go." Reaching across the stacked cases of water bottles, he gave her his last. "I kept two for myself, but y'all can have them."

"Finally, thank you." She twisted the cap to take a sip.

"You got it." He smiled.

"Everywhere you went, everybody kept laughing. Guess I should say they kept giggling. You were flirting with them, weren't you? What'd you say?" The woman asked boldly. "Lucky bottle because you're holding it." She used a deep voice to imitate Booker in action.

"No!" Booker didn't shout. It was intense and heavy laughter followed behind it. "I wouldn't call that flirting. Unless we're talking about that first group. I was definitely tryna get coug'd on." Booker admitted. "A couple of those groups, actually."

"That was more like making people feel seen. Maybe even heard. Now with you… oh I was flirting for sure. Why wouldn't I? Look at you." Booker nodded at her and shook his head in ways words couldn't explain then licked his bottom lip.

"That actually seemed sincere." The woman crossed her arms. Examining Booker, she wore a smirk.

"See… whatever I told them was what I felt needed to be said by someone if it wasn't being said already." He shrugged.

"OK, well that's fine. I mean… if cougars are your thing." Booker laughed while she continued. "But the whole 'lucky bee' thing, yeah… leave that one alone." She giggled, batting eyes as she walked away towards the food truck.

The woman's friend was getting her order and seasoning it the entire time. She missed their whole interaction. He could see them walking, talking, and looking back until they got lost in the crowd of people.

Booker was patiently waiting for his food, leaning on the stack of bottled waters. When Manny returned, he said, "That line was long as shit."

"It wasn't that many people when I got here, and they told me twenty minutes." Booker shared a similar experience in terms of time lost. "It's been at least that."

Minutes later, "Booker!?" Was called from the food truck.

Making his way to the pickup section, he took a wad of napkins. Some red and green sauce packets along with a couple forks. "Thanks," he said. Taking the food back to the water cases, he removed two of them. "I'ma have to drink purified water today."

"Ay, we used to drink it out of water hoses when we was lil."

"You aint lying. We drunk it straight from the faucet sometimes. My Granny's was up high on the side of the house."

"Savage." Manny said.

They laughed, divvying up the food. "Here you can take the bag. I'm gon put the tacos on top of these nachos and eat the street corn soon as we get where we going… Where we going?" Booker asked.

Booker and Manny searched for a spot for a few minutes when Booker noticed the Press entrance. "I might be able to get us in. You ever get a badge after the magazine work?" Booker asked.

"With the Big 3?"

"Yeah," Booker replied.

"Damn. Naw, I didn't. My bad, bro. I never got around to applying for one."

"It's smooth, I'ma see what they say."

Booker walked over to an opened section for media members and said, "Hey, I'm here with the Press but my friend doesn't have his Press Pass. Would he be able to come in off of mine?" He asked, showing the security his extensive media credentials.

"No, sorry. You can but he can't," the man said, bluntly.

Booker walked over to Manny and told him the news as they continued to search for a better view than what they found so far.

"They're opening up this section over here." The security guard pointed to a section right next to media row.

"Thanks!" Booker saluted the man as they walked in. There were a lot less people where they were for the moment. A number of others followed behind them and the area would soon fill. Booker and Manny stood two o'clock to the podium. The barricade was the only thing separating them from the media section.

"Crispy…" Booker held his thumb up, leaning against the barricade. He kept his word, devouring his street corn and everything else after. "I needed that," Booker said. "That's the first thing I ate all day."

"I had a big ass breakfast, so I was at about a half tank. I just needed to get back to full. I'm good now," Manny replied.

"It's," Booker looked at his watch. "1:36. I'm going to say they're getting started around three."

"Yeah, probably around then. People are still coming in. How many people do you think are here?"

"Three, four, five thousand? Shit don't get me to lying."

"I'm going to say about four thousand with another one or two on the way in. That line was long as shit, bro."

"That's what I'm saying. It's hard to tell. Who you think is bringing her out?" Booker asked.

"Big Gretch. Gotta be Big Gretch."

"I was thinking the same thang. A lot of people thought she was going to be Kamala's running mate. If that happened, bro… POTUS 2028. I wouldn't dropout but it'd be the loss of a lifetime. They'd steal all my voting base, bro. That'd be *all* the women."

"Every one of them," Manny confirmed, shaking his head.

Michigan's finest politicians from Governor Gretchen Whitmer, Senator Debbie Stabenow, and Senator Gary Peters. To the Midwest's Governors of the Blue Wall States all spoke their piece. As time went by, leaves fell from the trees with the blowing winds. Then the crowd went wild as the Secret Service agents got on stage and placed the Vice President's seal on the podium.

The applause carried over when, "Madam Vice President, Kamala Harris!" Blared over the speakers introducing the woman of the hour. Manny clapped with Michigan while Booker captured it all on the SD card of his 4K camera. Zooming in, he was able to get a bird's eye view of the event.

An overwhelming number of cheers for Madam Vice President, Kamala Harris led to her smiling, laughing, waving, and clapping with the people. She was left with no other option but to settle the crowd down by reminding them why they were there. "Thank you. OK, let's get to business. Let's get to business." She echoed, smiling.

"One day, bro. Again," Manny corrected himself. "It already happened in front of Joe Louis' Fist." He shrugged.

"If it happened once, it can happen twice." Booker reminded himself.

Madam Vice President, Kamala Harris began her speech to a captivated audience. Hearts were formed with hands. Phones were out in droves recording videos and taking pictures of Madam in motion. She was confident in her delivery and was very intentional in her message. "Because by the way, we will win…" she said calmly as the audience ignited with a round of applause, chants of *We Will Win,* and *Not Going Back.*

Catering to her audience, she also addressed the automobile industry that made the state of Michigan a 20th century automotive powerhouse. "We must and we will invest in the industries that built America like steel, iron, and the great American auto industry."

Booker and Manny looked at each other, both appearing to be thinking the same thing. "She's good, bro," Booker admitted.

"I mean she is the muh fuck'n vice president of the United States," Manny acknowledged as Madam Vice President Harris concluded her speech.

"In a democracy while we can hold onto it… Our vote is the power that each of us as an individual has. It's an extraordinary power!" She said with emphasis. "And we will not give it away, and we will not let anyone suppress or silence our power." She pleaded before passionately demanding, "Don't ever let anybody take your power from you!" The crowd roared as Madam Vice President Harris finished with a call to action.

"So Michigan today I ask you then… are you ready to make your voices heard?" She asked as they screamed and Booker yelled, "U KNO!!!"

"Do we believe in freedom?" Was answered by more thunderous applause.

"Do we believe in opportunity?" She questioned to even louder cheers.

"And when we fight…"

"WE WIN!" They all said in unison.

"God bless you and God bless the United States of America," Madam Vice President Harris said in conclusion.

Chants of, *WE WILL WIN* broke out as soon as she finished her speech as she replied, "Yes we will… I know… We will win…" calmly and confidently between chants.

Madam Vice President Harris smiled and waved goodbye. She exited, hugging stage mates, and waving at the audience before being escorted down the portable stairs.

"Damn, that shit was a movie, bro." Booker confessed, "We got *a lot* of work to do."

"A whoooole lot." Manny shook his head to agree as they walked towards the exit.

Over the next couple days, Booker was tagged in different posts on social media, streaming his antics from Madam Vice President Harris' Grand Rapids Presidential Rally. His phone was vibrating a little more than usual. But still it was nothing breathtaking. Most people didn't take his political campaign seriously anymore. Until momentum swung like a pendulum.

Ring, Booker's phone rang while he was in the zone, writing his live book *POTUS 2024*. Updating its contents with Friday's rally. Opting against ignoring it, he finished his thought and took the call from his Publisher. "Hello?" He answered.

"Hi, Booker. This is Janessa from LOTT, how are you?"

"Hey, Janessa. What's up?" He asked.

"Hey..." She hesitated. "Have you checked your email?"

"Uh oh. Naw, I haven't. Not lately. I've been in the zone finishing up POTUS. What I miss?"

"First let me say, you are one of the smartest, silliest people I've ever met. You and the higherups act the exact same." She laughed. "We've been getting so much traffic to the website and people asking what we do and who Booker Garvey III is.

"So, if you were trying to get some attention, you go, boy." She joked. "What made you get on that hill saying LOTT48203 like that?" She was laughing into the phone's receiver waiting on Booker's answer.

"I don't know, Janessa." He chuckled. "Nothing was working. I've been trying everything on this presidential run."

"I wouldn't say that. Most of the people who called, scanned the QR codes on their water bottles or something like that?" She questioned. "It's all in your active messages in the employee portal."

"Word?" Booker smiled at the rally's partial success.

"Yeah, and..." She paused.

"And...?" Booker asked by tone, wondering what was going on. By this time, Booker had walked all around his condo and was currently in the hobby room, fidgeting with his audio equipment.

"Annnd your speech from Hart Plaza was sent to us anonymously from an angle we haven't seen before and it's pretty polished. I didn't know there were news crews there, Booker. You made it seem like it was a bunch of Lions fans Downtown, recording on their phones."

"I thought it was just Lions fans. I didn't see any camera crews. Not on me at least." He chuckled. "I was feeling like the president already, that day. I can't lie to you. Everybody had their phones out, recording. I was still undefeated then. One and O. I'm one and ninety-nine now. So, I guess that's my base, Lions fans."

"That pity party is lit, Booker."

Booker laughed, "Hi-larious."

"But you're really two for ninety-nine. This video is free publicity. All we have to do is press the button. Do you want it out there? Joyce already has a press release written with the video linked. We're not a political party but we do air segments like this on the LOTT News Network all the time. Our resources are your resources, Booker. You're a LOTT Artist, now," Janessa reminded him.

"I'll tell you what. Watch it and try to get back to us within the hour, OK, Booker? Please do it now, Sir?" Janessa asked directly. "I'll hang up when I hear your voice in the background."

"You might as well let me watch it and get my response now because you know I'm terrible with emails and returning calls."

"You said it, not me."

Booker opened his email and saw a thumbnail of himself, crystal clear. Centerfold, yelling into his megaphone in front of the Joe Louis Monument. "Aw, this is cold. I can already tell," he said, pressing play.

"B GARV, POTUS 2024... out!" Went the computer speakers after replaying the video a second time. "Oh, that's cold. They got the Spirit of Detroit. The flag is in there and everything. Yeah, let's do it!" He answered with excitement. "Can you have the editing department run my promo page after I say *out* before you send it?"

"Absolutely. Anything else?"

"Nope, that's it. Thanks, Janessa."

"No problem, Booker, bye-bye."

Booker hung up and saved the video to his phone. He watched it several times in a row, deciding not to send it around. Instead, he waited to see if it'd be sent to him. Less than an hour later, his phone went berserk.

Running to the weight room of his condo, Booker started fist pumping in the mirror. "I'm back, baybeeeh!" He shouted. Thumbing through his text messages, that seemed to be never ending, he found Manny's.

M4nny
Today 7:04 PM

> You out here bro! Ride the wave! 🏄

>> Let's get it! That's bc we're 5-1 now! I told you bro, It's the jacket!

> Whatever it takes!

>> The office said the water bottle idea was a hit too, Campaign Manager!

> For real? Let's finish the job! We need a good follow up

>> What you thinking?

> Idk yet but it gotta be something big. That's the standard now. Anybody record what happened Friday?

>> Somebody sent that to US!

> Word???

>> Yeah bro. Somebody sent that to LOTT. They just put the LOTT News stamp on it

> Damn. That's what's up! You out here for real, bro. Silent investor???

>> Shiiiiiit, I HOPE SO!!!

> Ask and you shall receive! 😏

>> Please be a silent investor!!! Lbs! 😂🙏
>> Delivered

Booker went to sleep that Monday not knowing what awaited him in the morning. But things were starting to look better than they had.

POTUS 2024: BALANCE THE SCALE

Waking earlier than his alarm was a sign for him to get a good workout in before the bell. Opening his YouTube app, *Another day, another dollar. Thank the Lord for another twenty-four. God, I knew that was you,* played through the gym stereo system as the Bluetooth switched from his phone.

Putting on one of his workout playlists, Booker began bench pressing. Starting with a five foot, 30lb barbell then adding 35lb plates to each. Next, he added 25lb plates before replacing them with a set of 45lb plates and a pair of 5lb bumper plates, bringing the total to 200lbs. He continued to lift sets of ten, adding 20lbs to every set before stopping at 240lbs. For a quick warmup before finishing up in the evening.

A big breakfast followed his morning workout consisting of three eggs, four strips of turkey bacon, two pieces of turkey sausages, and a bowl of cheese grits. A shower and a change of clothes sent him on his way his way to work a little earlier than usual.

Entering through the back door, he was able to write morning work, change the date, set up breakfast, make copies, check his email, and open the attendance screen before the bell rang.

With it being almost time to greet students at the door, he noticed the hallway was abnormally quiet. A minute or so later, Booker walked towards the door wondering if his clock was off. Reading the watch on his wrist and his phone at the same time, he exited the door.

Booker was celebrated with a loud burst of applause from students, staff, and other teachers in the building. "We need to balance the scale!" The physical education teacher shouted, pumping her fist before stopping to blow the whistle hanging from her neck.

Booker was giddy for the moment as he embraced the support. He didn't know what to say. For a while he said nothing. Just saluted, smiled, and laughed at the handwritten signs, cards, and notes being passed to him by the student body. "Thank you," he finally said. A kindergartener gave him a picture of the two of them at the White House. "Thank you, thank you!" He repeated in doubles.

Funneling his way through the students in the halls, Principal MoVene walked and talked with him to the school's conference room across from the main office. "I know you can't wait to get back to work, but things kind of changed on a whim this morning. We're going to use your emergency sub plans and have Ms. Riske cover your class for the day. There are some people here to see you."

"Uh oh,"

"Nothing bad, I don't think. But they are higher ups. My boss' bosses are in there. You brought out the bigwigs, Mr. Garvey. From what I understand, you're getting ready to take a leave of absence to run your campaign. I'm not sure if that's what this is about but that's all I know and I didn't want you to be blindsided by anything. You know I'm upfront."

"Seriously?" He asked, raising his eyebrows while Principal MoVene shook her head in confirmation. "Thanks for telling me," he said, before opening the door.

Walking into the room, Booker had multiple thoughts and scenarios racing through his mind in a split second's time. Silencing them all, he trusted his gut. *Welp, this is what I asked for. So help me God.* He thought to himself.

The room was a who's who. Many politicians near and far. Local leaders to Governors were in the building to see what Booker was made of. Faces of stone from elder statesmen caught his attention first but would soon lose it. As peer and middle-aged politicians embraced him, eagerly awaiting his responses to everyone's questions.

An older, taller gentleman was separated from everyone with a woman roughly a decade younger. Yet aged so gracefully, she could pass for half her age. They stood alone conversing while the man watched a video on his phone, drinking a bottle of water.

A group of women Booker had been talking to brought him their way. "Mr. Garvey, this is Mr. Van Sertima and his Partner, Mrs. Clarke. We'll let you talk in peace, now," the lady said, walking away carrying a clipboard. Her high heels clicked against the floor at a steady pace. While Booker's eyes stayed strong to avoid looking at her behind. She was a curvaceous woman, and he could only hope to see her again.

"Hello, Mr. Garvey. I'm Isaac Van Sertima. This is my Business Partner, Advisor, and Assistant, Mrs. Jasmine Clarke. We've advised and managed one hundred forty-three successful campaigns with one hundred thirty-four of them resulting in victory. We are winners, Mr. Garvey. That's why we're here. We're at the point now where we pick and choose and no longer accept new clients. However, we were moved, Mr. Garvey."

Booker was very engaged by the man's pitch, but he didn't know how to respond. The moment was becoming bigger than himself. "Your speech was very moving. Spontaneous. But very moving. One of a kind, guaranteed. We also saw you at Madam VP's rally last weekend and connected the dots because of your megaphone. We like your passion, Mr. Garvey, and your fire," the man said, boldly.

"We *need* more passion in politics. Liking what we saw and seeing you were still at it; we gave you a little nudge to see what'd happen. We were able to get footage from one of the news stations who was there covering the draft." Booker's eyes lit up.

"We don't have to talk dollars and cents until you're elected but I can give you an estimate further down the road if you like."

"How much are we talking, roughly?" Booker wondered.

"It's not about the money, Mr. Garvey. It's about the White House. We are not cheap. I will say that. Consider it a backend expense." He suggested.

Isaac held up his pointer finger as if he forgot something, "Speaking of time, Mr. Garvey; something we do not waste. If you don't win, we'll pay you the presidential rate for *your* time," he said.

Isaac pointed at Booker in a serious manner and Booker no longer knew what to say so he tried deflecting. "I was just curious. I have a Campaign Manager and Advisor already, but we could definitely use your experience on the team." Booker offered.

"With all due respect, it has to be all or nothing. Your Advisor and Campaign Manager can join our staff in other roles. We'll need as many people as possible around that you trust that we can get." Jasmine explained.

"Campaigns get ugly, Mr. Garvey and when it rains… it pours. Too many cooks in the kitchen can ruin a counter full of fresh groceries. Which is why we politely decline your request." Isaac reasoned.

"Here's our card. Think about it." Isaac handed Booker a business card. "We have a tentative campaign trail set up throughout Michigan and the West Coast. But your political career with the Realist Critical Thinking Party starts Thursday if you accept.

"Your participation with RCTP needs to be confirmed by o'six hundred, Thursday. Look everything over. We'll give you a call in the morning and go from there. Sound good?" He asked.

"Sounds good." Booker shook the extended hands in front of him.

"Pleasure meeting you," Isaac said.

"Thanks for your time. Nice meeting you," Jasmine added.

"Pleasure is mine, thanks."

Booker smiled as the woman with the clipboard returned with the group. "How are you feeling, Mr. Garvey?" She asked.

"Booker, but you can call me, Book. I'm feeling good. Ms.?" Booker queried, tilting his head with a half-smile. Licking his bottom lip habitually.

"*Mrs.* Jarreau. Sorry, I didn't introduce myself. You can call me, Monica, *Mrs.* Jarreau, *Mrs.* J. Doesn't matter to me." Sliding papers underneath the clipboard to free her hands, she said, "I'm Mr. Van Sertima and Mrs. Clarke's Assistant. I do all of the bookings and scheduling." She paused to shake his hand.

"This is Mrs. Julene Stevens." She introduced a woman with long, curly, dark brown and gray hair. She's our Operations Director. She deals with the people-side of things. HR stuff.

"Mrs. Lenice Princeton, our State Director is in charge of where we'll be running things on a day-to-day basis when we set up a location in the community. Ms. Claudine Sommers is our Director of Communication. She handles contacts and the media side of it all. She also keeps eyes and ears on things being said about you in smear campaigns and social media. It gets ugly, Mr. Garvey."

"I heard." Booker shook their hands and his head.

"There's a lot of other people to meet but we'll introduce them as they come. The Party is the team Isaac and Jasmine assembles for an election campaign. That's who you'll be working with directly after signing your contract. Us, The Party.

"Well, we told the Board of Education we'd get you back to them by ten o'clock and we don't do things late. We run on real time here, Mr. Garvey." She looked at him over the top of her glasses as she slid them up the bridge of her nose.

Monica escorted Booker back towards the entrance area where the Board of Education, the district's superintendent of schools and other administrators waited patiently. With new leadership at the helm in the district office, Booker sat in front of them not knowing what to expect. "Good morning, Mr. Garvey. I believe we met during a school visit last year when I was hired in. I'm Dr. Samuel Dalton. I've heard a lot about you Mr. Garvey."

"Yes, I remember. Nice to meet you again."

"Of course. Mr. Garvey, we wanted to talk to you in regard to your decision to run for office. We saw your video on TV and social media and although it is motivational, we have to ask you to drop out of the race or resign from your position."

"For what?" Booker asked quickly. "I've been here twelve years now."

"Taking office is a big, time commitment and we have to prioritize the needs of our students first."

"If my teacher ran for president, I'd feel invincible. If he can do it, I can do it. Especially in October. The race is almost over," Booker countered.

"I understand, Mr. Garvey. With the M-STEP and other testing coming up, our students need a teacher who'll be here and present."

"Dr. Dalton, the only day I've had to miss this year was today and that's because I was pulled from class to be here with you."

"Mr. Garvey, we've made up our minds. Either drop out of the political race or resign from your position."

"Dr. Dalton, Board of Education, and other Administrators, I won't be doing either. I'll be filing paperwork for a sabbatical and when I get elected, don't expect any favors." Booker shook his head and pushed his chair in. Closing the door behind him, he exited the building without bidding farewell to anyone at the table.

Walking to the parking lot, he remote started his truck while his name was being called. "Mr. Garvey!" Dr. Dalton called from behind him.

Turning around, Booker's face soured realizing who it was as he continued walking to his truck. "Mr. Garvey, wait."

"Dr. Dalton?" He acknowledged.

"Sorry about what happened back there. My hands were tied. The Board made the decision at an emergency meeting last night. I was just the bearer of bad news. Believe it or not, I fought hard for you. So hard, I probably should've lost my job. I think they were waiting to see if I'd actually tell you."

Booker seemed surprised by what he heard, "Yeah?"

"Tempers flared, that's for sure. Good call on the sabbatical and on the fly too. You're sharp. Presidential shit right there." Dr. Dalton extended his hand.

"Yes sirrr!" Booker chuckled, shaking his hand in truce before walking away. "I'm headed to the district office to file the paperwork, right now."

"If they end up firing me, you think you could find a job for me on staff?" He joked.

"Uh, yeah! Let me know." Booker saluted Dr. Dalton as he opened the door to his truck. Rolling down the window, "I'm serious," he said, then pulled off.

Dr. Dalton shook his head up and down, raising his hand as Booker drove away.

Booker spent the rest of the day with his phone turned off. He unplugged from the world and focused on the next couple weeks of his life. Moving into the early evening, it was time for Booker to, "Plan, plot, strategize, and bomb first. Boom!" He rapped along with the song banging through the sound system of his condo. He held his first two fingers like the barrel of a gun on each hand. Wearing a leather vest, gold rope chain, a Rolex link bracelet and matching ring on his middle finger. Without a shirt. Booker was really feeling himself.

"Give me my money in stacks!" He shouted, throwing twenty, fifty, and hundred-dollar bills in the air; jumping around, speed walking, and bopping through the rooms of his living quarters. Booker performed a full-fledged concert to 2Pac's hit records while his interviews played on the 100" 4K QLED TV mounted to the wall.

Making a trip to the kitchen, he grabbed a gallon of water from the refrigerator and drank from it at the island. In front of hanging pots and pans, *Put my right hand to God...* the speakers blared as Booker raised his right hand. Nodding his head to the song's beat, he played an imaginary trumpet with the horns of the chorus.

Taking a seat, he picked up where he left off as one of his workout playlists played its last song. Jotting down thoughts and ideas, he wrote names of everyone he trusted and what roles they were capable of filling. *Campaign Manager... Manny or Van Sertima? Manny is my dawg but that's not even a question.*

"Hmmp." Booker chuckled. *But how do I even know they're legit?* He thought to himself. *Should I play hardball?*

Tossing his phone into the air, he thought about plugging back into the matrix. Deciding against it, the phone dropped on a couch pillow.

Activating the Siri feature in the upper right-hand corner of his MacBook, Booker asked it to, "Google, Isaac Van Sertima."

Picking up his TV remote, he pressed a button, saying, "Alexa, Google, Jasmine Clarke," he spoke into the Smart TV remote control. "Damn!" He shouted, impressed by his findings on both screens.

Staring off into space, Booker was having an epiphany. "I got it!" He shouted, clapping his hands on the way to the master bedroom.

Changing into his workout attire, Booker walked over to the condo's *Fitness Center* to finish his workout from the morning. The main room was a large lounge area with a pool table, arcade games, a dart board, axe throwing lanes, a couch, loveseat, recliner, TV, air fryer, and mini fridge.

There was a lofted twentieth and a half floor above it all for the third bedroom. Each of the three bedrooms had glass ceilings over the bed for star gazing.

The perimeter walls and bedroom ceilings were made of glass with remote controlled tint and frost options. The frost appeared to be opaque on the outside while offering full city views to its occupants inside.

Most rooms had different floor textures and were separated by half walls. Egyptian rugs over the carpet in the living room and bedroom. Marble for the bathroom and kitchen. The dining area and hallways, buffed hardwood floors. Rubber mats covered the

Fitness Center's floor. Located in the center of the condominium on an elevated platform.

Taking the Bluetooth, sound canceling headphones from a hanging hook in a small locker cubby. Booker put them on and found a playlist to listen to. Next, he put on a pair of elbow sleeves and wrapped his wrists before working out.

Racking a 7ft, 45lb barbell, he warmed up by lifting the bar ten times before placing a 45lb weights on each side. Lying on his back, he grabbed the barbell and pulled himself up off the bench and back down. Booker planted his shoulder blades on the bench. Driving his feet into the ground, he lifted the barbell off the rack, completing another set of ten reps.

Then he hit on a heavy bag in the corner for a minute before returning to the weight bench.

Adding 25lbs to both sides, he finished his tenth rep before heading over to the speed bag for a minute before his next set. Removing the twenty 25lb weights, he added 35lb weights and pushed the bar up another ten times. Breathing heavy, Booker grabbed a jump rope and began hopping at a slow, steady pace. After a minute, he returned to the rack for another set.

Removing the 35lb plates, Booker grabbed the handles of a second set of 45lb weights hanging from the weight tree. With two 45lb weights on each side plus the barbell, his total was 225lbs.

For his last set, he added 25lb weights to each side to bench press 275lbs. He was bench pressing more than he weighed by 70lbs for ten reps. Breathing heavily through his mouth, he pushed nine tough reps. Booker yelled pushing up the last rep, "Ahhhhh! Ten! Mutha fucka!" He shouted.

Sweating through his clothes, he removed his shirt and hung it to dry inside his locker. Walking to the Fitness Center's shower booth, he rubbed his stomach thinking of what to eat to help repair his sore muscles. In the meantime, he ripped open a 5oz pack of tuna and ate it like the crumbs of a bag of chips. Stripping down to skin level, Booker got in the shower for twenty minutes and washed his body from head to toe.

Stepping onto the floor mat he dried off. Putting on a pair of boxers, Booker got his headphones to do some writing while it rained. Torn between the soundtrack of thunder and lighting, he put on the headphones and listened to some jazz instead. "Play, *Kind of Blue*," he said into his phone.

Snapping from the zone he was in the midst of, he stopped writing to make a trip to the refrigerator when a knock beat on the door. The knock continued and grew louder while the doorbell rang.

With the kitchen being on the opposite side of the condo, Booker was completely oblivious to it all. A key entered the hole and slowly turned as the door opened. Feet of familiarity searched the bedroom first, then the office. Next, eyes peered out the window to the greenhouse on the patio. Then finally they headed to the kitchen.

Closing the door as the figure turned the corner, Booker looked as if he saw a ghost. "What the damn!? You can't just walk up in here like that. It's tools all around this muh fucka. C'mon now." Booker looked confused. Wondering if he was in the right place himself, he contracted his eyebrows, waiting to hear what was going on.

"I… I…" She paused, laughing at herself. "I'm just glad you're alright. I thought something happened to you," she said. Her shoulders drooped and her neck muscles loosened, dropping her eye level in height.

She folded her arms saying, "I texted and called you all day Monday after your video went viral again. Then I thought, maybe he's in the zone and has been writing all day trying to finish the book on time. Or maybe he missed my calls in between everyone else's.

"Then I texted this morning and called and it kept going to voicemail, all day. I checked your social media, nothing. Then somebody told me you got fired and I really got worried. I said, OK. If he doesn't call me by five o'clock, I'm going over there to see if he's lying on the floor, half naked, smelly, and drunk… or worse."

"Worse?"

"I don't knowww," she dragged out. After Lina's long vent, she began to feel concerned again as her eyes watered.

Finally exploding, she sobbed hugging Booker. "I thought something bad happened to you." Crying as though it did, he comforted her with an even more confused look on his face above her head.

"You alright down there?" He asked.

"Yeah. I feel so stupid." She laughed, wiping her tears with the bottom of her palms.

Booker chuckled. "Something happened, that's for sure. Nothing bad though and I didn't get fired." He laughed this time. "Damn near probably because they def wanted me to quit."

Catching her up on things, "Wow!" Was all she could say.

"That's all you got to say?"

"What am I supposed to say? You just lived a whole movie in twenty-four hours." Lina laughed. Her puzzled expression made Booker more intentional with his questioning.

"Well, what should I do?"

"Call Mr. Vanhower and Mrs. Clarkson, duh." She joked, hunching her shoulders. "They seem legit but what if you win?" She asked.

"I got it all planned out. Well, outlined. I'm ready, now. I wasn't before but with *Van Sertima* and *Clarke*," he emphasized. "I gotta have a gameplan. I can't show up unprepared even though I just started this plan after my workout."

"There you go. Well, I'll let you finish. I was just making sure you were... OK. I'll let you be."

"Wait... hold on," Booker said, gently grabbing her hand. "How about you *let me be* in a little while." He flirted. Pulling her closer, he kissed her soft, cocoa butter coated lips as they embraced each other. Bumping against the walls of the structure, they hugged and kissed all the way to the bedroom.

Up and down, around and round their bodies were in sync. When hearts collided, they made a steady beat. Their privates danced under the beams of light shining through the windows of the master bedroom of the condo.

A nap brought him to mid evening hours with a recharged battery. He was refreshed and ready to take on the world. Walking to the kitchen, Booker followed his nose to an all too familiar scent. "Do I smell fries? I hope that chili goes with some dogs. I'm not calling them shits glizzies!" He rejected, shaking his head.

Booker smiled as Lina prepared his plate in the nude. "Ooh we! Heaven... Must be missing an angel," Booker sang, shirtless.

"I figured I'd feed you before I got out of here. I just wanted to make sure you were OK."

"I am now. Ahwoooooo!" He howled.

"You are so silly." Lina laughed, hitting him with the towel she was holding.

Food and conversation wrapped things up between the two which led to the continuation of Booker's workday. Lina walked to the bedroom to get dressed while Booker stayed for seconds. "I weigh two o'five! I have to maintain my figure. Look at me now… Don't tell me that ain't a perfect specimen of a man," he said, impersonating Muhammad Ali.

"Mm hmm." Lina agreed, smiling. "Well, Champ," she said, I'll see you later," she added, fixing her clothes in the mirror. Standing on her tippy toes, she lifted herself to give Booker a kiss before leaving.

Booker began shadowboxing after she left to get his juices flowing. "Back to business!" He shouted, clapping his hands. Sitting down at the kitchen island, he continued his list of names for potential Cabinet members.

Coming to a stopping point, he circled back to Campaign Manager. It was the last position left blank. "Isaac Van Sertima with Jasmine Clarke," he read aloud as he officially etched their names in pen. Booker had solidified his plans and teammates for the biggest play of his life.

Flipping his pen to the table, he walked to the living room. Opened his laptop and tunneled down a YouTube rabbit hole on pruning cucumbers.

Waking from his sleep, the lights of the hallway chandelier was the first thing he saw. Booker groaned and rolled over, keeping his eyes closed as he came back to reality. Searching for his phone to check the time, the screen read 6:55AM then it rang.

This muh fucka thinks he's Morpheus and I'm Neo. Booker thought, reading the *732* area code across the screen. "Hello?"

"Mr. Garvey?"

"Speaking."

"This is Isaac Van Sertima. How are you?" A familiar voice greeted. His distinct accent separated him from most people who were calling him without a name tag.

"Great, sir. Thanks for asking. You?"

"I'm well. I won't hold you up this late in the morning."
Late? Booker mouthed to himself.
"Mrs. Clarke and I were wondering if you gave the things we spoke on some thought?" Isaac asked, cutting straight to the chase.
"Yes sir, I did. I'm ready when you are," Booker said, boldly. Fully believing in the path he was preparing to trek.
"A day early. Excellent, Mr. Garvey. Excellent. I understand you're on a sabbatical?"
"What happened to confidentiality?" Booker asked, in wonderment.
"It is public information now, Mr. Garvey. It was announced at last night's School Board meeting."
"You were there?"
"I wasn't but *we* were. We're everywhere, Mr. Garvey."
"If one is there, we're all there," Booker replied, realizing he was talking to one of his own.
"Hmmp," Isaac sounded. "I knew it. What Century Club if I may ask?" Isaac was seemingly relieved talking to a member of the same sociopolitical organization.
"I'm not surprised either." Booker laughed. "Not one bit. MI7.1 2015. You?"
"NJ7.1 1965."
"A point one from the sixties." Booker nodded his head. His face adjusted to the times and he was careful what to say next about them. "I know you've seen some shit."
"Stepped in it too. Too many times."
"I can't wait to trade war stories."
"We'll have plenty time to trade war stories, Mr. Garvey. Especially with the road trips and flights across country. We have a nice amount of cities and states lined up between now and November fifth."
"So, is today my first day now?" Booker asked, recalling their previous conversation.
"Technically, yes. Today is just a briefing. Tomorrow, we're headed to your hometown for some camera work. Saturday, we have a rally to attend. Sunday, you deliver your first speech in Detroit. Next week, you deliver that speech five times in five cities. We're going to start off light and see how it goes."
"Light?" Booker repeated, laughing aloud.

"When things get rolling, Mr. Garvey, you'll be delivering speeches five times in five states."

"POTUS 2024."

"Yes, POTUS 2024. I just wanted to follow up with you, Mr. Garvey. Now that we know where you stand, make sure to get plenty of rest tonight. It may be one of your last chances to get a full night of bed sleep for a while. Tomorrow will be a long day and the campaign trail starts Monday at o'six hundred. You've been emailed the specifics."

"Six… AM?" Booker asked for confirmation.

"The early birds win elections, Mr. Garvey."

"Prize Fighter. You read my book!" Booker laughed, greatly impressed.

"True indeed. Very well written. All your books are. When I saw you up there on that hill, I knew exactly who you were and was internally ecstatic. I've been wondering how your brain was wired for some time now.

"Good day, Mr. Garvey. Check your email ASAP. You'll need to be prepared. Any questions about anything?"

"No Sir, I think we're all set here. I appreciate the support, Mr. Van Sertima, I mean that. I'm not just saying it."

"Not a problem. Call me Isaac. We're partners now. Don't take anything I say personally. I'm a straight shooter. Anything else wastes time. We don't have time to waste. We actually need time. We have to make up for lost time.

"Kamala is the current vice president and Donald is a celebrity entrepreneur turned president. I'll be frank. Current expectations for anyone joining the race this late is to lose and lose badly. Two scenarios with us, win now or at worst in four years with the publicity gained from this year's run. Plan on the former and latter. Just in case. We are winners, Mr. Garvey and winners, win."

"Damn right!" Booker exclaimed. "And call me Booker. We're partners now." He chuckled.

"Very good, Booker. Don't mind if I do. Good day. See you tomorrow."

"See you tomorrow. Peace." Booker hung up the phone.

Laying his phone on the side table next to the living room couch, Booker took a deep breath and put his head in his hands. His forehead had perspired. Sitting up straight, he wiped it off with the back of his hand. Standing from the couch, he stretched and changed clothes for an early morning workout to start the day.

After warming up for ten minutes with a weighted jump rope, Booker slipped on a pair of Air Max '97 running shoes. Then he walked down twenty flights of stairs from his penthouse condominium to the building's main lobby. Setting off on foot, Booker ran downhill to KL Ave. Towards Western Michigan University's Main Campus.

Arriving to the roundabout at the campus' entrance, he circled it before heading back to his condo. Racing uphill towards the building, Booker emptied the tank running as fast as he could for the last leg of his run.

Reaching the top of the hill, he put his hands on his head to open his airway. He paced back and forth, catching his breath.

"Who is that?" He heard a visitor ask his neighbor.

"That's Booker. Stay away from him, girl. Nothing but trouble. I've seen more walks of shame from him than the lobby in Hoekje. Shit… I was one of em," she said with a lookoff. Turning her head away to fix the hair behind her ear.

"Ooooh," the woman added. Raising her hand for a high five.

"It was all good just a week ago." Booker shook his head with a look of glum.

"A week?" The woman's friend asked.

"Girl, boom. It was four and a half years ago, and we are not going back." They laughed, clapping hands. "He wishes."

"I really do, Peach." He smirked. "Your friend too."

Biting her fingertips, smiling. The woman waved.

"Girl!" Peach hit the woman's arm before pulling it down.

"Sorry, Booky. Those days are *over*."

"So, why'd you call me Booky?"

Puckering her lips with attitude as soon as he started talking; she folded her arms, squinted her eyes, and shifted her bodyweight to say, "Book-er. I said Book-er! Ugh. Bye!" She waved him off as they scurried inside from the patio.

"Girl, you better get him. Look at him." The woman motioned outside with her head. "And that smile. Those aren't veneers either, girl. He has a gap."

"Uhn unn. Why you all up in that man's mouth?"

"Because *you're* not."

"Girl, stop. You, *better* not." Peach pointed at her as the patio door closed.

Laughing to himself, Booker walked over to the bike rack to unlock his and took a ride to cool down. Riding around the basketball court of the condominium, Booker ended up riding through the water sprinkler with his hands up high like he won a race. Feeling loose again, he turned around and headed home.

Locking his bike to the rack, he jogged up twenty flights of stairs to the penthouse. After a shower and post workout meal full of protein, Booker opened his laptop to get an idea of what to expect for his first week in politics. Reading his unopened emails, he finally came across one from *VanSertimaIsaac@RealistCTParty.org*

Skimming through the email, he couldn't believe his eyes. "What!" He shouted after reading, *TV 33: Thursday, October 24, 2024, at 06:00… Twenty cities in five days.*

"C'mon man! That's not light, dawg. Dayyyyuummm!" Once again, Booker found himself trying to figure out what he had gotten himself into. Sitting in his Lazy Boy recliner, he let out a long, deep, sigh.

XI: Third Party

Waking from his sleep before his alarm, Booker felt refreshed beginning his morning routine. With a little time to spare, he reached under the bed for a set of 15lb dumbbells. A three-minute nonstop bicep workout was on the menu. The break between sets were shrugs.

It was an exercise done without resting the weights and afterwards, his arms were on fire. Stretching as he walked it off, it was time to start the day. The cold marble floors of the master bathroom stabilized his six-foot frame. His barefoot toes braced his body as he made his way to the cabinet underneath the sink.

Removing gray, T Liner Andis clippers, he lined up the edges of his tapered haircut. Cutting against the grain, he freshened the blended sides of his beard.

Teeth, Flossed and brushed. A washed face led him on his way to get dressed. Turning on the lights to the master bedroom closet, he searched high and low for the day's clothes. "Alexa, play: Last Time That I Checc'd."

"On it," Alexa replied.

Phluuudddddddd, a money machine counted. *LAST TIME THAT I CHECKED!*

Booker danced as he filed through shirts and pants for the big day. Realizing he was in the wrong section of the closet. He walked over to the opposite side for his dress attire. Removing a black suit and tie, he kept it simple. Completing the look with a pair of black dress socks and Concord 11 Retro Jordans.

"My fellow Americans." He practiced while adjusting his tie. "My fellow Americans, My fellow Americans, My fellow Americans." Booker repeated over and over in different tones of voice until finding the one that fit. "My fellow Americans," he commanded in a familiar tone. Shaking his head with a smirk, "Yeaaaaaah," was all he said next.

Walking to the kitchen, Booker read Isaac's email to verify the pickup time for his departure to the TV station across state. Booker opened the French doors of the refrigerator for an apple and a gallon of water before heading out.

Pressing down on the elevator call button outside his door, Booker entered as it opened. Slowly, he walked back and forth, rehearsing his speech. The elevator bell rang on the first floor below his in the twenty-story building overlooking the city on one of Kalamazoo's tallest hills.

Standing at the elevator door was a mother and child who were headed somewhere before the school day. "Hi, Mr. Book…"

"Shhh, Mi Mi. Don't speak to him anymore."

"Mommm-mmy…" The little girl whined.

"Be quiet, Mi Mi." The woman instructed with her pointer finger.

"Brenda, I'm sorry." Booker held the elevator door open.

"You are sorry," she said, looking him in the eyes before turning away to press the down elevator button. "Tell Mr. Booker, bye-bye, Mi Mi."

"Bye, Mr. Booker!" The little girl shouted, smiling.

"Bye, Mi Mi!" He smiled, waving as the doors closed. "Damn," he whispered to himself. "Fuckin heartbreaker," he added. Making his way to ground level, the elevator bell dinged again on the third floor. "Aw shit, part two," he said, looking at his watch.

As the elevator doors opened, Booker was halfway smiling in anticipation of who he might see next. To his surprise, she was not alone and his face soured. "Hey Booker?" The woman said, acknowledging his presence.

"What's happening, Peach?"

"Nothing much, headed to the gym. Why are you in a suit? It's not even six o'clock yet," she said, looking at the time on her phone.

"I got a TV spot in Highland Park."

"You love yo lil bitty ol city." She laughed.

"Chill, chill." Booker chuckled. "Don't forget about Brightmoor. Fenkell is on the West Side too. I ain't one of y'all but

I appreciate y'all for taking care of me while I stayed there," he said. "So, give my city its propers like I give y'all its!"

"Whatever. Oh, this is…"

"Kendrell." The man shook Booker's hand, firmly. "*Shantel's* boyfriend."

Squeezing the man's hand with added pressure, Booker felt Kendrell lighten his grip. "Booker," he said in a deep, dry, monotone voice and nodded. The elevator door opened, signaling the end of a unique introduction.

Walking through the lobby, Booker saluted the doorman as he exited the building. Checking his email once again, he read the license plate of a black, 2023 Mercedes Benz Sprinter parked ahead of him to make sure they matched. "This shit is really… happening," he said under his breath as he approached the vehicle. A middle-aged man exited the driver's side, reaching for Booker's belongings. "Hello, Mr. Garvey. I'm Norman." He shook Booker's hand. "The Chauffeur these days. Keep what you need, and I'll take the rest."

Norman opened the door for Booker, then placed his duffle bag in the back of the vehicle. Stepping into the Sprinter, "Oh my damn." Slipped out like a hiccup.

"Act like you've been here or wherever we are, Booker." Isaac said. "But it does look nice in here, huh?"

"Yeah, this looks like a legit office."

"I designed my portion. Mrs. Clarke has done the same with hers. Yours is in the back. You're going to need that corner for sleep more than you know."

"I'm sure. The dividers are dope too. What is this, bamboo?"

"Yes, actually." Jasmine answered. "And no, you won't." Jasmine stepped in front of Booker before he sat down."

"Mrs. Clarke, you don't want any problems I bring from knee knocking. You'd get us both in trouble with that big ass ring on yo finger."

"Negro, please," she replied.

"Here comes Jazz," Isaac said, calmly watching it all with intrigue.

"My youngest son is your age. I have bras your age. You're a baby to me," she said, sincerely. "I need your shirt and jacket. This is a two-hour drive," she said, reaching underneath her desk for a couple hangers and a garment bag.

"Damn," he said, humbly. Booker unbuttoned his oxford and was left sitting on the bench alongside the window in his A shirt.

"If the cameras were rolling, would you be ready?" Isaac asked as Norman pulled off.

"Of course, it's ShowTime."

"Alright, action. Let's hear it."

Since I was in 5th grade, Mrs. Witherspoon's class, back at Barber Elementary in my hometown of Highland Park. I can recall having presidential aspirations. I was born during the Regan administration. Raised during Bush's, grew up during Clinton's and another Bush; I was a college kid during Obama's run, speechless with Trump and disappointed in Biden.

Which is why I'm using this forum to announce my candidacy for president. Why me? You may ask. I was born in a city that no longer has a school district or library... it still has citizens. Highland Parkers.

A city like so many others where some students are living house to house, couch to couch, shelter to shelter. While some students were born with a literal silver spoon in their mouth. That's no one's fault but—

"Is this the same speech from draft night?" Isaac interrupted.

"Should it be something different?"

"You have the right delivery, but that video went viral. People want to hear something new. A remixed version. You're old enough to know about remixes."

"A different version than the original song."

"Precisely. You can use the space in the back. There's an intercom to reach us. A laptop and briefcase with supplies and instructions regarding setting a passcode for the lock. You have two hours total. But we need to hear the condensed, yet inflated version in thirty minutes."

"Got it."

Booker went to the back of the Sprinter and had a seat on the bed and desk area of the vehicle. The back of the Sprinter was made like a bench bed. The arms of the bench flattened to make a bed. While the front of the bench extended like a recliner with the touch of a button, adding to its width. "This is cold," Booker said in amazement.

"Act like you've been here and everywhere we go, Mr. Garvey," Jasmine reminded him. "Talk like that when we clock out."

"Yes ma'am."

"Jazz."

"Booker." He smiled. Opening the briefcase, he removed a notebook and ballpoint pen then opened the laptop. Opening the Google Doc, he began revising his speech. "This might be a stretch but is there a printer?"

"Wrong mindset, Booker. The question to ask is, *where* is the printer? You need to expect there to be a printer." Jasmine taught him. "Presidential expectations. There's a QR code for Wi-Fi and the printer on the desk."

"OK! OK! OK!" Booker clapped. "Act like I've been here and everywhere until we're off the clock," Booker reminded himself. "Check!" he said, counting to one on his fingers. "Presidential expectations, check-check!" He counted two on his second finger.

The first ten minutes of the ride, Booker hadn't changed a word. He didn't know where to start. Straightening the hairs from his mustache to down his beard, he started carving letters.

"Time," Isaac said with his timer beeping. "Take two." Isaac pointed at Booker.

Since I was in 5th grade, I can recall having presidential aspirations. I was born during the Regan administration. Raised during Bush's, grew up during Clinton's and another Bush; I was a college kid during Obama's run, speechless with Trump and disappointed in Biden.

Which is why I'm using this forum to announce my candidacy for president. Why me? You may ask. I was born in a city that no longer has a public school district or library... it still has citizens. Highland Parkers.

My high schools, plural, were both demolished and never replaced. Yet I still reached my educational aspirations. Once upon a time, I was the Prom and Snowcoming King. So, imagine how civil peace talks would go with me at the helm.

"Please cut that." Jasmine laughed.

"Dayyyyuuummm. I thought that was gold. You know? It shows people voted for me and I stood the test of time."

"It shows you live in the past. What have you done lately, Booker? Nothing old please. Unless it's meaningful. If you were class president and it was the start of your presidential aspirations, still nobody cares but at least it's relevant."

Booker nodded his head, agreeing. "Your biggest support groups may not have even enjoyed high school. You have to always consider the majority. Bankers, Lawyers, Judges and other politicians want to know why you, too not just Highland Parkers."

After high school, I went to Wayne County Community College, WC3 for short. Then my car was stolen from my driveway three weeks after I bought it for $2,800. I saved $1,400 and my parents matched it when I was working at Radioshack on 12 Mile and Woodward at nineteen.

That's where I worked after leaving my high school jobs at McDonalds over there on 6 Mile and Livernois and the Joe Louis Arena Little Caesars. That's partly why I announced my campaign at the monument.

It was Subway before that in HP. I worked hard saving for that car working at Radioshack where I ranked 6th in the district signing up customers for cell phone contracts when I was nineteen... But after those bandits stole my car, I needed a fresh start.

"Stop. You can cut all of that." Jasmine waved, shaking her head left to right. "It's unfortunate, but it's unrelatable to the masses and doesn't really fit anywhere."

"Shit." Booker laughed a little, rocking from the bumpy ride.

"Hey, it is what it is." Jasmine hunched her shoulders with a straight face. "Go ahead."

Booker looked at the words on the page, mouthing them to himself for a few seconds before continuing.

Western Michigan University was my next stop where I pledged my fraternal alliance to Phi Beta Sigma, Zeta Delta Chapter. Shortly after I graduated with a Bachelor's degree in Elementary Education, I taught 3rd grade for seven years and fifth for five. That's twelve years of work with the youth. Again, imagine how civil peace talks would be with me at the helm!

"OK, wait." Jasmine held her hands out, stopping him again. "Cut the frat boy line too. You don't want people seeing you as the Party Boy. Let people find that out you're a Sigma. You don't see me, *Oo-oop'n,* making triangles all over the place, do you?" She asked, striking a pose, forming a triangle with her hands by her hip. "But!" She stopped. "Keep the last line about your teaching experience."

"I knew it! You Devastating Diva you!" Finally understanding the mission at hand, Booker was back to the editing room.

"Be more specific about balancing the scale. What initiatives are you going to introduce? Tell the cameras about two or three of your biggest plans or problems you'll address," Isaac added from the front of the Sprinter.

"Check!" Booker confirmed.

The bench bed had drawer slides on the side of it and wheels that locked. The table ahead of it folded into thirds that pressed against the side of the vehicle. A remote controller allowed Booker to fold the table by tapping another button. Options were also available to control things ahead of time via app.

Wheeling closer to the desk, he entered the zone needed to finish his speech in the next seventy minutes.

"Alright, check this out," he said, walking to the middle of the moving vehicle to have a seat on the bench by the door.

Since I was in 5th grade, I can recall having presidential aspirations. Why me? You may ask. I was born in a city that no longer has a public school district or library… it still has citizens. Highland Parkers.

My high schools, plural, were both demolished and never replaced. Despite those obstacles, I hurdled them on my way to Western Michigan University where I earned a Bachelor's degree in Elementary Education. I taught 3rd grade for seven years, 5th for five. That's twelve years of experience working with our youth. Imagine how civil peace talks would be with me at the helm.

I went from East Michigan to West Michigan then back east where I got a Master's degree from Eastern Michigan University in Education Administration with a 3.7GPA while teaching full time. I'm also a writer. The greatest Writer of my generation. The greatest Writer of my era, the greatest Writer of the 21st century.

Timeless stories of perseverance can be found in my first novel, Michigan International University along with children's book, Wake Up Little Lion. Like detective stories? REAL detective stories? Read about the rise to fame in Rydon Tyme: Nobody Cares, Bad Move, and Prize Fighter. Want to know how I am as a teacher? Grab a copy of First Day of School. So far, we have readers in thirteen countries worldwide. How? LOTT Magazine was a part of that. So imagine, again, how civil things will be with me at the helm during peace talks already having relationships with other countries.

To the media machines, no propaganda or smear campaigns. I'm an open book. All of my original takes and any responses to allegations I catch wind of will be aired on LOTT News Network. Check www.LOTT48203.com for all official campaign announcements and updates.

My plan is simple: Balance the scale. That's our campaign slogan. Balance the Scale! Some countries like Canada, my neighbor growing up. In 2022, the entire country had 874 tragic homicides. In the same year Chicago, Illinois suffered 695 tragic homicides. Right here in Detroit, 309. That's

POTUS 2024: BALANCE THE SCALE

1,004 lives lost way too soon and that's just Detroit and Chicago! We need to balance the scale!

Some children grow up bouncing around from house to house, couch to couch, shelter to shelter. There's an estimated 60,000 families who are homeless right here in America. Not 60,000 people, 60,000 families. Which is about 30% of the entire homeless population. Students! While you have some children who grow up with a literal silver spoon in their mouths. They didn't ask to be here. They didn't ask for that. You brought them here. But that's not the point. The point is we need to balance the scale!

If this is to be one nation under God, then we need to act like it because the devil's agents and non-believers are working hard as hell… We need to balance the scale!

B GARV, POTUS 2024… Out!

"It's a start," Jasmine said, nodding her head.

"Eh." Isaac was uninterested. "Keep in mind, you're not talking to Lions fans as a Lions fan this time. You're on TV. If people don't like what they hear, they *will* change the channel. Or go to YouTube," he reminded him.

"Was it that bad?" Booker asked.

"It's not that, these are the days of eight point two-five second attention spans," Isaac answered. "You have to say interesting things or sound interesting. Tone inflection. Capture your audience like Martin or Malcolm. Even 2Pac. He didn't say *Feel me*. He said, *FEEEEL ME!* The people need to *feel* what you're saying."

Booker nodded his head, chuckling.

"Marvin Gaye sang differently every album it seemed like. 'Trouble Man' does *not* sound like 'What's Going On?'"

"The numbers you gave about homelessness was new news to me. But that's what it felt like. The news. We need to *feel* the impact of knowing that thirty percent of the homeless population are families." Isaac concluded.

Booker continued shaking his head as he returned to his workstation. "It's not what you say but how you say it. We're thirty-five minutes out. Do with it as you may," Jasmine chimed in from the front.

Rehearsing his speech under his breath over and over again, Booker was starting to find his groove. He could be heard at different parts and not at all during others. He was getting back into the zone he just departed. "Alright, we're ten minutes out," Jasmine announced, reaching for Booker's shirt.

"Remember when I asked if the cameras were rolling, would you be ready?" Isaac asked.

"Yessir!"

"By that, I meant…" Isaac used his hands to find the words he wanted to say. "There'll be camera crews outside the station before we make it in. They'll be looking for an interview on the spot. So be ready."

"Aw shit, y'all are full of surprises."

"That's the world we live in," Isaac reminded him.

"Stay ready, you ain't gotta get ready!" Booker shouted.

"Very true."

Booker began putting on his shirt as he was told, "You have to learn how to work the camera, Booker. How many presidents have you lived through that were physically in shape?" Jasmine asked.

"Obama?"

"And he's a buck sixty, tops," Isaac replied.

"Show your muscles man," Jasmine said as they turned down Victor Street. "Two minutes!" She said, lifting her voice. "Here, Isaac," she said, handing him Booker's suit jacket. "When Norman opens the door for you, *then* start putting on your shirt. You need exposure and a voting base. As of now, we're targeting single women, single mothers, and women as a whole."

"Shit, me too." Booker laughed.

The Sprinter arrived in front of the TV station and as promised, there were ten to fifteen media members from all over Metro Detroit awaiting their arrival. "ShowTime." Isaac announced, patting Booker on the back as Norman exited the Sprinter to let them out.

As soon as the door opened, camera shutters closed like opportunities. Booker stepped down, getting dressed in what seemed like slow motion. "Must've been hot in there?" One reporter asked, breaking the ice.

"I think it's just me. I tried jogging here, but they picked me up in Battle Creek." Reporters laughed as they took notes.

"Hal Saunders, Detroit Gazette. Mr. Garvey, what makes you think you can manage a country full of people coming from managing eleven-year-old fifth graders?" He squinted, confused.

"The forty-fifth president of this great nation became president after firing people on TV. I can't fire students. I can suspend them for a day at most and make recommendations. But I can't fire them. So that means I have to solve problems and not just push them to the side. If he was able to put experienced politicians around himself, you better believe I'll do the same. The best of the best." Booker nodded his head forward, pointing at one of the camera lenses.

Jasmine and Isaac stood behind him, nodding their heads in approval while Isaac tapped Booker to help him put on his jacket. Sliding his arms through the sleeves, he hunched his shoulders for a better fit. "Alberta Roberson, Highland Park Sun. Are you a Politician or a Model?" She asked.

"Both, actually. Glad you asked. The A shirt I'm wearing with the Michigan Mitt on it can be found on our website. That's www.LOTT48203.com/shop."

The crowd of reporters laughed at his remarks. "Gia Portis, Dearborn Beat. If elected, what do you plan to do first?"

"First, I'll be putting together the most dynamic Cabinet ever assembled. Next, for my first one hundred days in office, I'll be visiting all fifty states every other day. I'll be meeting with the Governors of those states.

"I'll also be meeting with four mayors from each state and two superintendents. The four Mayors will be those with the highest and lowest grossing economies. The other two Mayors will come from the highest and lowest populated cities in those states.

"The superintendents will be from the highest and lowest ranked districts in the state. I'm old school. I don't believe in recreating the wheel. We have tremendous leaders all around the country and I'm going to find them all.

"I'm not a Talent Scout at *Leaders* of Tomorrow, Today for no reason. We've been preparing for this day for twelve years. We *find* leaders of tomorrow… today," he said, high on confidence.

"Sorry, everyone. We have to go. Booker has an interview right now with Talk Beat. You can catch that on TV 33 Highland Park-Detroit. Thanks," Isaac announced as they pulled Booker towards the entrance of the building.

Pressing the buzzer, the Office Manager opened the entrance gate for the trio while Norman handled parking. The woman at the desk looked stunned. "Hello," Booker said, waving.

"You look just like my youngest son. Wowwwwwwww," the woman said. "Oh, my goodness. We all really do have a twin out there somewhere. The woman asked for a picture and proceeded to call her children on FaceTime. "Let's see what his Dad, Brother and Sister say. He's teaching so he may not answer."

"Really? I'm a teacher too!" Booker added. Wondering how close the resemblance would be.

"Look who I'm with," The woman said, holding her phone.

"Ali! What are you doing here?" A woman asked. "Wait, that's not Ali. you look just like my little brother." She laughed. "That's crazy."

"That's not Ali." A man laughed with her. "But he does look just like him. You got something to tell us, Ma?" He asked, laughing again.

"Not unless I had twins who were separated at birth without me knowing. Now your Father better not have anything to tell you all."

"I know that's right!" The woman on the phone chimed in.

"Hello?" A deep voice said, answering the call.

Hey Dad
Hey Dad
Hey Dad

Laughing a deep, loud, hearty laugh, the man said, "Don't even try it."

Coming into the call late, was the man of the hour. The woman handed Booker the phone to see his response. Booker and Ali looked at each other like a Spider-Man meme of them pointing at each other. "That's AI?" Ali asked. "I hate AI."

Everyone laughed unexpectedly. "Yo brother from another mother." The woman continued laughing.

"I was about to say, the only AI we acknowledge is Iverson and Iggy."

"Iguo-dala!" Booker shouted in a unique tone.

"They both silly for no reason too, look like," the man said on FaceTime.

Laughing again, the woman said, "I just wanted you to meet your twin. He's a teacher turned Writer too. He's from Highland Park but grew up on the West Side. I'm reading his profile now. This is really weird," she admitted.

"What's good… new bro?" Ali asked in confusion as they all laughed.

"Wassup new bro," Booker laughed. "Teachers unite!" He shouted with his fist balled.

"Teachers unite!" Ali laughed, balling his fist.

"I thought you'd be teaching and couldn't answer."

"I just dropped them off to Art. That's fifty minutes. I'm at the gas station next door. I had to grab a water," Ali said, holding up a gallon of water.

"OK, Well I'll tell y'all the details later, but I had to call so this man didn't think I was a stalker. Bye, y'all." The woman smiled and waved at the screen.

Bye Ma
See you Ma
Bye
Alright nah, Mama! Aight new bro

"Bye! Aight, new bro." Booker laughed, saluting the screen.

"That was wild," Jasmine admitted.

"Boy, I tell ya," Isaac agreed. "Erie."

After sharing another laugh, the woman introduced herself to the group, "I'm Ashele, by the way."

The group shook hands as she guided them down the hall. "Is there a restroom nearby, Ashele?" Isaac asked.

"Coming up here on the left." She motioned.

"Thank you, how long before showtime?" Isaac asked.

"There's thirteen minutes left on the current show with a five-minute break between shows. Just under twenty minutes."

"Perfect. Here, Booker. Put this on," Isaac said, handing him a black LOTT polo shirt. "Remember when I asked if the cameras were rolling, would you be ready?"

Laughing ahead of what was next, Booker replied, "Yup. Second time around. Stay ready…"

"You're catching on quick. Right now, you're here as Booker Garvey III the author. Remind people who you are before we hit the campaign trail.

"Ohhh, OK. I thought y'all changed the speech to today on me." Booker looked relieved.

"No, no, no. That was just practice. The speech is still on for tomorrow." Isaac assured him. "Do you have anything you're working on that you're at liberty to talk about?"

"I actually *just* signed with LOTT and I haven't released anything since Prize Fighter. POTUS is my first book with LOTT. I usually bring books with me to interviews and TV spots. I thought this would be all politics. I feel a lil unprepared."

"Don't," Jasmine said, handing Booker a brown, leather messenger bag. "Everything is politics."

Opening the bag, he smiled as he removed some of its contents. "Stay ready so you won't have to get ready," he said, finishing his mantra. "Five copies of each book." Booker smiled, shaking his head. Removing one of each book, he handed the bag and books to Isaac as he left to change shirts.

Pictures of the studio owner hung from the walls along with pictures of him with celebrities from then and now. Opening the door to the floor set, "You two can have a seat here." Ashele pointed to a waiting area off camera. Then she walked Booker to the set.

Walking in last, with a brown fedora and matching suit was the talk show host. "Hey Ma'am, I didn't know your son was in town. My man!" He shook Booker's hand.

"Talk Beat, this is Booker Garvey III." She laughed. "We all just got off FaceTime with Ali. He wouldn't have believed it if he didn't see it with his own eyes."

"Who would?" He chuckled. "Nice to meet you Mr. Garvey. You ready to do this thang?"

"Yessir!" Booker answered.

"I'm going to get it started, then I'm going to turn it over to you and let you do your thing."

"OK, good deal," Booker replied.

"Whichever camera has the red light is the one you're looking at. We come in after the break." He said, preparing Booker for the moment.

"We're live in three… two… one…" Turbulence, the show's Producer called out from the backroom.

The theme song played through the studio's sound system while the host drank from his coffee mug. "We're live!" Turbulence yelled from the back.

"Hello! I'm here with." He paused, motioning for Booker to pick up where he left off.

"Booker ahem Garvey III," he said, clearing his throat.

Jasmine and Isaac looked at each other, hoping for the best as the reintroduction show kicked off. Booker hadn't interviewed since before the pandemic but quickly knocked off the rust when asked why he started writing. "It was a form of release therapy. Things that I was going through during the day. If it was a real frustrating day, I could get that stress out on a keyboard. But at the same time, I was able to start a second career," he said, beginning to answer the question.

"It really just started as a blog. My friend… and this is kind of to anybody who's thinking about chasing a dream or getting into writing. He was telling me to blog—" Booker gave background knowledge on what a blog was before continuing.

"He said start with a blog because you never know where it'll take you and from that blog, I ended up writing eleven books. I was the Editor of a magazine—"

"Well hold on now, hold on, hold on," a deep voice interjected. "You've got sooo much. You've got so many things going on," the host said, highlighting some things Booker glossed over.

The interview went on for almost an hour. Before it ended, things got serious. "Tell me, there are children. There are adults… How can they come together. What will allow them to come together, so that the children can feel greater feelings towards education?"

Booker listened intently. He was processing what he heard in real time before giving a genuine, earnest answer. "We gotta kind of break our ways. We gotta get out of the way that we're living now." Booker suppressed laughter from a full circle moment in the middle of his answer.

"I was listening to Ball of Confusion on the way here and he said, *Nobody's interested in learning but the teacher*. We gotta change that. We gotta get outta that. We gotta make learning cool because that's what I used to call myself. 'A cool a– nerd' That's how I classified myself. We gotta make the nerds, cool. We gotta find a way to make the right thing, more realistic. More fun."

Booker went on about his thoughts of making learning a better experience for all students. Before they knew it, it was a wrap.

"Great job, Mr. Garvey." Talk Beat shook Booker's hand. "That was like a football game. I just threw the ball up and you caught it for the touchdowns," he added. "Hey, the seat is yours anytime you want it Booker Garvey III," Talk Beat said. Gathering his belongings, he left the studio in time so that the next live show could setup before showtime.

While commercials played over the network, Jasmine walked over, nodding. Then fist bumped the front of Booker's knuckles. "Not bad, Booker. Not bad at all. You started off a little rocky during the introduction, but you landed that plane.

"It was insightful, too. That's what this was about. Putting your ideals and beliefs on record before the ball gets rolling. Good job, man. You'll need to carry this momentum over into the speech."

XII: Speech!

Being on the road from city to city, Booker's phone was starting to go haywire, all day every day. From family, friends, old friends, college friends, high school friends, childhood friends, work friends, friends-friends; to people he barely knew or not at all. Having the same number for twenty years had its pros and cons.

There were a few numbers he hadn't seen in some time, meaning it was Booker's turn to reach out. "Mr. President! What's good?"

"Manny, I'm cool'n, brodie. I been meaning to hit you back sooner, man. But everything took off so fast. One minute I'm talking shit on top of a random ass hill. Next thing I know, I'm getting recruited by a whole ass political party. Bro, the shit is wild." Booker explained.

"I ain't trip'n, mane. I can only imagine how it is. When they aired yo shit on the news before the game, I knew somebody put some kinda bread up."

"I didn't know what the fuck happened, bro. LOTT told me it was sent anonymously. After it went baby viral again, it brought out the big dogs."

"Naw that wasn't baby viral. You were on the news, bruh. All the stations." Manny corrected his oversight.

"My dawg." Booker chuckled. "I get to work, the school quiet as a muh fucka. I ain't know what was going on. I went in the hallway and the PE teacher was dancing like a got damn scale. Bouncing left to right. The shit was wild, bro. I'm telling you. That was Tuesday. The fastest three days of my life. Easy!" Booker shook his head.

"That shit sounds crazy." Manny laughed.

"That's what I'm saying. Ay, I was hitting you up for a reason. Kamala and Chelly O is coming to Kzoo tomorrow. You tryna roll?"

"Yepper. Lettuce!"

"Bet, it's gonna be a lil different this time. These muh fuckas know when it's starting. They said between four and five, so we don't have to get there until three they said. Calm as a muh fucka, bro. Then they tell me shit like, *Act like you've been here or wherever we go.* How, Sway!?" Booker shouted.

"You a funny muh fucka, bro." Manny laughed hysterically. "Ay, I told you *one day* at the last rally."

"You did but that was just last Friday." Booker laughed again. "Isaac emailed me about this one with Madam Vice President and the First Lady. That's dawg who got the Joe Louis Fist speech pop'n again. He said they got the footage from one of the news crews there. Crazy they all had footage and never aired it."

"Right, that shit went social media viral then. It's everywhere now."

"See what I'm saying? Now all of a sudden everybody wanna play it on the news. Where the fuck was y'all at when we were passing out waters? Or when I was up on that hill getting booed." Booker laughed at the past.

"Dawg. That shit was hilarious! I couldn't laugh though because I woulda been up there with you if I ain't have to keep our spot in line."

"That was a wild ass day." He remembered the times. "Ay, I'ma hit you up when I wake up Saturday because if you don't come with me, I already know I ain't gon be able to get you in. Isaac and Jasmine don't run on CP time. Not even a little bit. Everything is scheduled."

"Bet!" Manny laughed.

"Aight mane. I'ma holla at you."

"Alright, bro. Peace."

"Peace!" Booker shouted, pressing the end button. With one down, he still had two others to call as he started tapping the screen.

"Hello?"

"Hello, can I speak to you?"

"Here you go. Hi, Booker."

"Damn,"

"What do you want me to say, Booker?"

"You know shit dun change, Lina. C'mon now. Look at the TV," he said, getting to the point. "I can't een lie to you though. That popup creeped me out a lil bit. Especially coming in like that."

"I knew you were going to say that. I was knocking and ringing the doorbell for a few minutes first. It just felt different than any other time we hadn't talked in a while.

"Like now, with all the missed texts and calls. Even though I just wanted to congratulate you. I knew you'd call one second before I was ready to let Booker be Booker."

"Damn, Lina. Look, one day I'ma have all the time in the world to give you."

"I never asked for that, Booker. I just said check on me *sometimes*. At least make me *think* you care. I was with Charlotte from the Burnhams one day. I saw her at the Greek picnic a couple years ago and we've been cool since then. Well, we were getting smoothies yesterday and I called you… voicemail. You know how she is, so she insisted on calling you to cuss you out on your voicemail… Booker, you answered the phone full of energy. Booker, what did I do?"

Booker could hear Lina crying over the phone and started rubbing his forehead. "Lina, I know it looks bad, but we talk about different things. I can talk to her pretty much anywhere. I need privacy when we talk."

"I get it but how do you think that makes me look? Forget look. How do you think it makes me feel, Booker?"

"I can only imagine."

"Yeah, well I don't have to imagine."

"I'm going to text her right now."

"It's not that serious. I just wish you showed you care more. *If* you care." She pointed out.

"I do care, Lina. You know that. Time just goes so muh fuck'n fast but that's no excuse. I'ma try more. Shiiiiiit, what you doing Saturday? Kamala Harris is bringing Michelle Obama here, tomorrow. Wanna be my date?" He requested.

"I heard about that. I wish I could but I'm going home tomorrow to see my family. I'm so mad I'm going to miss it." She pouted.

"Chi Town! Damn, me too. We'll make it up. When you get'n back?"

"Probably Tuesday."

"OK well, I'll talk to you Tuesday?" Booker asked.

"Uhn hum. We'll see."

"Sholl will! Bye and goodnight. I'ma send you a kiss emoji to put somewhere."

Lina giggled into Booker's ear. "You put it somewhere whenever I see you again. Bye, Booker."

Smiling, Booker took a trip to the fridge before making his last call of the night. The change in circumstances also changed his approach to the situation. Leaning on the counter, he took a seat at the kitchen island and made the call.

"Mr. President?"

"Kenya, Kenya, Kenya," he said, shaking his head. "You make it sound so good."

"I didn't do anything, it's all in your head."

"You're all in my head."

"I was hoping you'd make me smile today." Kenya giggled into the receiver.

"Shit, me too." He chuckled. "Why? What's wrong?"

"Michelle Obama is coming to Kalamazoo but when I went to register it was full. I tried right before you called." Kenya pouted.

"Come with me," Booker said, sporadically.

"Noooooooo."

"Why not?" Booker laughed in relief.

"I will save you your *I did not have sexual relations with that woman*, speech."

Booker laughed so hard; he dropped the phone. "What cho ass say!?" He asked, imitating two comedians at once. "You funnaaay!" Booker continued laughing.

"I'm serious. You're hot right now. Whoever you're seen with will be your woman without a ring. Tabloids would make a comeback off of your butt."

"Well, let them think what they want."

"Uhn un." She rejected quickly. "If I'm going to be getting caught up in sex rumors, I'd at least like to be having sex with the person."

The phone line went silent for a few seconds while the two registered what was said. "I'm glad one of us said it…" Booker said in a deep, low tone.

"Book-errrr." Kenya dragged out the letters in his name.

"Did I say too much?"

"—" She paused before saying, "No."

Booker and Kenya continued talking for another hour before Booker started calculating hours of sleep needed to function at a high level in the morning. "Kenya, sweetheart. I gotta get some sleep. These muh fuckas *start* the day at 5:00AM with me coming in at six, real time. They do *not* operate on CP time. I keep telling people that." Booker reasoned. "I won't be surprised if they pop up early."

"You are so silly." Kenya laughed. "It's OK, Booker. I understand. Goodnight."

"Goodnight. Hopefully I'll be able to say that in person when this is all over in a couple weeks."

Kenya giggled again before hanging up the phone. "Byyyyeee, Bookerrrrr," she said, seductively.

Booker was high on life. shaking his fists in front of him, all he could do was smile. Preparing for bed seemed a little easier with his political career stabilizing.

After a long night's rest, Booker modeled his outfit inside the full length, tri-fold mirror at the end of the front hallway, underneath the chandelier. Corduroy pants, wheat Timberland boots with a brown peacoat laying on the bench against the wall. After brushing his head, he wiped pieces of hair from his T-shirt before putting on a light brown sweater.

Making his way to the kitchen, his phone rang. "Yoooooo!" Booker answered the phone.

"What's good, bro? I'm in the lobby."

"Bet, I'll send the elevator."

Booker pressed two buttons on the kitchen wall, back-to-back. The first let the doorman know his guest was approved and the other sent down the penthouse elevator. It was a smaller elevator that was located next to the others in the lobby.

The lobby elevator and Booker's penthouse elevator gave him four exits out of the condo. The other two being the back stairwell on the building's west side and the emergency exit in the master bedroom's closet, north wall.

Manny rang the doorbell as his face appeared on the kitchen monitor. Booker pressed a third button on the wall that unlocked, opened, and closed the front door. "Mr. President! What's good?" Manny shouted, seeing Booker step outside the kitchen.

"What's happening, mane?" Booker asked, shaking Manny's hand, and snapping his fingers after.

"I can't call it. You look happy. You got that Bruce Leroy Golden Glow."

"I feel like I got a chance again man. Kamala might still be a problem. But it feels like I got a muh fuck'n chance again."

"That's all you can ask for."

"Dawg," Booker agreed.

"You got a chance to steal votes for real this time. People know who you are now."

"We gon see. Ay, I really brought you here to get you back on the team, dawg. I felt bad replacing you as Campaign Manager."

"C'mon now, man. I feel honored to have been replaced." Manny laughed, shaking Booker's hand. "I don't know nobody else who'd run for president to even have a chance to be a Campaign Manager, bro. It's all good. I'll be the muh fucka who gets donuts." Manny paused. "Aight, maybe not him but the one who tells dawg to get the donuts." He laughed.

"Naw, naw... fuck that." Booker chuckled. "Claudine Sommers. She's the Director of Communications. That's yo shit anyway. I should've been thought about this. She hasn't hired anybody yet because this is technically only my third day. You can run the social media accounts as Head of Content if you want to. That's a good ten bands, bro, and it's less than two weeks. The days are long as a muh fucka though."

"Shiiiiiit, I'm wit, bro! I keep telling you this." Manny shook Booker's hand. They slapped palms twice before saluting each other.

Ring, went Booker's phone.

"Hello?"

"Booker, are you ready? We're outside," Jasmine asked.

"I can be." Booker read two o'clock sharp on his wrist. "Give me two minutes."

"Take five," she said as they hung up.

"Bro. Real time. They're here a full hour early to make a fifteen drive. Maybe I need to take notes."

Booker grabbed a blazer and tossed it to Manny. "Throw this on over yo hoody, G. I don't feel like hearing they ass because they will cut into both of us like it's nothing!" He shouted, contracting his arms.

Walking out the front door, Booker hit the button to the building's three primary elevators to make their trip downstairs. As the tinted, sliding lobby doors opened, Manny noticed, "That's the same Sprinter from the Ru."

"You *did* say something about a Sprinter with black rims, and snow tires. But those ain't snow tires. I don't know what the fuck they are, but they ain't snow tires." Booker laughed.

Getting into the Sprinter, Manny was amazed. Skip, hopping as he walked around, *Oooh* and *Ahh* was all he said. "Ooh, is this bamboo?" He asked, Feeling its shellacked texture. "Ahhh, ay that desk-bed is *crazy*. Ooh wee! Look at that TV," he said, noticing the vehicle's multifunctional tinted windows. Part of it served as a mirror with rest being used as a fully functional, touchscreen monitor with Wi-Fi access. On the outside, the windows appeared to be completely blacked out.

"OK. Who's going to say it? Or is everyone waiting on me to do it?" Jasmine asked the group, low on patience.

"Manny! Ay, bro. Look at this." Booker went to the back of the vehicle to show him the mini fridge he had installed inside his desk. "Ay, you gotta act like you've been here or anywhere we go from here on out. Or they gon make me boot yo ass, bro. These muh fuckas ain't bullshit'n, G." Booker could only shake his head. He was jokingly serious.

"Damn, aight. You right. Playas fuck up too."

Manny got himself together and started over with a proper introduction. "Manny." He said shaking Isaac's hand. "Manny." He repeated, politely shaking Jasmine's.

"This is Manny, y'all. He was my Campaign Manager. I'm going to talk to Claudine about getting back to his expertise. He was a Communications major. He'd be great for the Head of Content position."

"Sounds good. What has he done?"

"He's got a good five thousand followers on IG." Booker informed them.

"Are they spending any money?" Isaac asked.

"They spend any money?" Booker looked over to Manny.

"Naw, I just post for memories pretty much."

"Like a personal page?" He asked.

"Yeah."

"OK. That's between you and Ms. Sommers." Isaac was out of it.

"Where's your camera?" Jasmine asked him.

Booker hung his head realizing he forgot his own camera and quickly tossed Manny his company issued iPhone 16 Pro. "Use the LOTT line."

"That works if you know what you're doing with it. We'll see what you do today. If you make magic, I'll talk to Ms. Sommers about it myself. Monday morning when the rest of The Party flies in."

"Sounds good to me." Manny smiled, shaking his head.

"Don't worry about posting anything yet. Everything goes to the Cloud. The Video Editors and Social Media Marketing Team get them straight from LOTT phones and cameras. Most of the cameras have Wi-Fi. They'll edit and post whatever you approve with the caption you send." Booker instructed.

"Bet."

"When they send you a copy of whatever it is that they post, switch accounts and post it on the RCTP's page."

Booker showed Manny the gadgets he recently had installed in the Sprinter during their ride to the Wings Event Center. Booker tapped Manny's arm, signaling him to walk to the front of the Sprinter with him. "I thought it'd be busier than this," Booker said, looking at cars exiting the freeway at Sprinkle Road. "I mean *clearly*, it's a lot of people but I thought it'd be bumper to bumper. Where's everybody parking?"

Manny pointed to a line of cars turning into a large parking lot for a flooring factory located across the street. Large groups of people were walking from the parking lot to the event center.

"What kind of tires do you have on here?" Manny's question was running rampant in his head.

"They're made from a soft, recyclable rubber like material that doesn't require air. They just need to be replaced every hundred thousand miles. We don't have time for flat tires, Manny," Isaac answered. "Any other questions?"

Manny shook his head as they turned down Vanrick Drive. Norman slowed down to speak with a couple of officers who stopped them because the street had been barricaded. After a brief conversation, Norman showed an ID card that was scanned along with the vehicle's VIN number.

Norman got out of the vehicle and opened the door with a member of the FBI who let everyone know, "I need to scan y'all's ID before we let you through."

Everyone obliged and they were on their way to a private parking lot further down the street. Booker and Manny smiled from ear to ear, having a flashback from last week. "Act like you've been here and everywhere we go. You lose a lot of leverage in the political world when you fan out. Fan out when you clock out." Jasmine reminded them.

"My bad, Jazz." Booker apologized.

"You better believe I'm going to fan out when I clock out over First Lady Obama. We've crossed paths several times through the years. But I haven't seen her since she's been First Lady and it's always been in passing."

Walking into the east entrance of the event center, the group entered first. Manny came in last, capturing it on camera in spurts.

Avoiding any amount of heavy foot traffic, they were able to take their time along their walk to the elevator. Getting off on the top floor, they followed the bend along the wall. Isaac scanned an ID card, unlocking the door to one of the suites. Isaac held the door as they walked in with Manny trailing to capture it all.

Booker walked in last before Manny, biting his cheeks to hide his smile. He straightened his mustache and goatee to conceal it. Jasmine sent a stern warning between her eyebrows knowing what was next to come.

Knock - Knock, knock, knock, knock – Knock, knock, knock. went a knock at the door as Manny put his phone away. Jasmine smiled at him.

Norman opened the door for an older gentleman who appeared to be in great health and high spirits. "Norman. It's been too long," the old man said in a low serious tone, shaking Norman's hand.

"It has been a while, Bronson." Norman smiled, shaking Bronson's hand.

"Everything good?"

"I can't complain. I really can't." Norman replied.

"It wouldn't change anything. I've always liked that about you, Norman. We'll catch up later." Bronson pat Norman on the back.

"Yessir." Norman nodded at Bronson.

"Hey Dr. Grove." Jasmine smiled from the soul, shaking Bronson's hand with both of hers.

"That's my great grandpa. I'm Bronson. I keep telling you that, Angel. How's your Aunt, Mother and Father?"

"They're good, Bronson. I'll tell them you asked." Jasmine smiled.

"Isaac."

"Bronson."

The men greeted each other with a strong right handshake. Hitting each other's biceps with their offhand, they were happy to see each other.

"Booker!" The old man said enthusiastically. "You look different without your megaphone." Bronson turned to laugh with Isaac and Jasmine. "Nice to meet you, young man. I've heard great things."

"Nice to meet you too, Mr. Dr. Bronson, sir."

"Unbelievable," he said. "Bronson. That's all. Just Bronson. We're all here to witness history. What does my doctorship have to do with anything?" He asked the room as it grew silent.

"Exactly." Getting straight to the point, Bronson looked Booker eye to eye.

His eyes had bags that had seen the world. Hair sprouting from his nose and ears filtered many stories, fact from fiction through the years. With election season rolling around he only wanted to know one answer, so he only asked one question.

"I've got $250K for this campaign... if you can tell me your plans to help big businesses." Bronson shook Booker's hand again.

"Whatever you say, I'm not going to hold you to it. I'm going to hold the Realist Critical Thinking Party to it and if you deliver, they know me." He looked back. "That ticket gets higher. But if you bullshit me, Booker," Bronson said, intensely. "Then I'm through with all the Realist Critical Thinking Party's candidates for the next election. We clear on that?"

"Crystal clear, Bronson."

"Good. Now, I didn't say you *had* to deliver but I *expect* you to make a sincere attempt with whatever you say next. Don't bullshit me, Booker. What is your plan to help big businesses?"

"As much as I want to say, block all international trading, and go back to the days when most things said, *Made in the US*. That's pretty unrealistic."

"I understand."

"What I will promise is to balance the scale with our promotion of our country's bigger businesses. A lot of attention goes to small businesses as it should. But the Fords, Chevrolets, Chryslers, and Grove Air and Automotive Companies are the backbone of this country because you all built it by making it mobile. We're a moving society now."

Bronson shook his head as Booker continued. "If I can't get tax cuts or any other kind of incentives passed through congress for American based companies. Then I'll shoot commercials with Fortune 500 companies. Starting at the top. If they block it, I'll endorse them subtly during appearances." Booker said, sincerely. "Except spirits, firearms, and some other things I can't promote as president."

"I like it. Good answer. *Great* answer." The old man signed and dated a check that he wrote to the Realist Critical Thinking Party for two hundred fifty thousand dollars. "Well, here's a piece of advice." Bronson ripped the check from his checkbook.

"It should explain where I'm headed next without my saying so. Never put all your eggs in one basket, Booker." Bronson shook Booker's hand before handing him the check.

"But I have a feeling my next stop will cost me a lot more than $250K. It was nice meeting you."

"Isaac, Jasmine, Norman, always a pleasure and you Sir, pardon my manners. Bronson." He shook Manny's hand.

"Manny." He nodded his head subconsciously.

"Manolo. That's my brother's name. Nice to meet you," Bronson said before departing.

The Party left the suite, shortly after Bronson. Walking down the hall, Isaac and Jasmine gave Booker his congratulations while Norman pressed the elevator button. Entering the elevator, they briefly recapped what happened in code.

"That's rare air you're flying in Captain. Don't expect to fly at that altitude every flight," Isaac said.

"Yes sir!" Booker shouted, looking at the check one last time before handing it to Jasmine as the doors closed.

Making their way to the standing room only section in front of the stage. Norman handed the Secret Service agent everyone's credentials while Manny captured it before putting the phone away. They stood near the stage's entrance, next to the walkway for nearly twenty minutes. All of a sudden, the small crowd backstage began moving towards them with everyone taking pictures and videos.

Looking to see where to go, First Lady Obama followed the Secret Service Agents leading her to the stage's entrance. Michelle Obama was making her way to the podium when Booker shouted, "First Lady Obama!" Pointing repeatedly to Jasmine with both hands as she walked out; Jasmine stood in front of him, ignorant to it all.

Her shoulders hunched until First Lady Obama saw Jasmine and lit up, smiling and waving. Jasmine was caught fanning out when First Lady Obama put her hands together before continuing her walk, clapping. Jasmine was waving ballistically, jumping up and down while Manny recorded the moment.

First Lady Obama slowly walked out to a deafening, one minute standing ovation that ended early at her request. "Thank you," she said, over and over again, smiling, waving. At one point, she seemed mind blown by all of the waves, cheers and screams of support and appreciation.

First lady Obama put her hand over her heart then both hands together and thanked Michigan for their support. "We want to get this show on the road. Especially for our folks standing here in the Mosh Pit." She shared a healthy laugh with the Great Lake State.

Soon after Mrs. Obama started her speech, The Party made their way to media row, where they had tables set up on an elevated stage. News channels from all over the country were doing live broadcasts as they walked to their section. Manny recorded their entrance, zooming in on the sign saying, *Reserved for the Realist Critical Thinking Party* before pocketing the phone for a moment.

They were just behind the floor seats. Who were just behind the standing room only section in front of the stage. "But most of all, I want to thank all of you. Because..." First Lady Obama stopped mid speech to address someone she locked eyes with, in the audience. "Oh, one hundred years old? No, oh my goodness. You look amazing," she said, talking over the applause.

Manny had been recording already and zoomed in on the section. "Ay, LOTT News has a table down there. I'm about to grab a Nikon. You want one or you gon stick with that?" Booker asked.

"Next time, yeah. I'll keep using this to keep it all together," Manny answered.

"Fasho, I'll be back," he said, walking behind the scenes to check out some hardware. "Hey, how you doing? I'm Booker Garvey III. I'm a LOTT Writer and I need to check out a camera. If you have any extra." Booker opened his wallet to show his work badge.

"I know who you are, dude. I'm Porcha. LOTT News: West Michigan. What do you shoot with?"

"Honestly, I always just grab a LOTT Bag—"

"Nikon or Cannon?"

"Nikon,"

"I have a Nikon case. What's your go to?"

"It was the D5300 then I start using the D7500 and kinda stopped using my old shooter."

"It happens, dude. I'm using a Z9. Both of those are in there and I won't need either. The check out log should be in there. If it's not, let me know."

"OK, thanks."

"Yeah, no problem."

"Do you have an extra tripod?" He asked.

"You can check out anything in the case, dude. I have everything I need already."

"Cool, thanks."

Booker returned the RCTP's table with a Nikon D7500 and a lens strong enough to reach the stage with clarity. Setting up the tripod, Booker focused the lens on First Lady Obama before returning to his seat. Isaac signaled him over. Booker sat down and leaned closer to hear what Isaac had to say.

"Notice how the First Lady has everyone's attention."

Booker looked around the arena and saw everyone was invested in what Mrs. Obama was saying. "It's because she's telling one helluva story. You're an author, right?" Isaac asked.

"Yeah."

"So tomorrow, when it's your turn... tell them a story." Isaac smiled and nodded towards the stage for the First Lady's next line, "A woman's body is complicated business y'all," she said, igniting laughter of relief from the audience. "Every woman here knows what I'm talking about," she said as the women in the audience agreed and applauded as the crowd joined them.

Mrs. Obama didn't end without challenging the state of Michigan. "Let us not just sit around and complain. Let's..."

"DO SOMETHING!" They all shouted.

"If you have an aunt who's thinking about sitting this one out or voting for a third party." Booker's jaw dropped.

"Why do you think she said that, after seeing who... when?" Isaac questioned, raising his thick, salt and peppered colored eyebrow. "You're a big dog, now... dawg."

"If people weren't thinking about voting for a third party, they might be now," Jasmine added. "That's a silent endorsement. She threw you a bone."

"Now *that's* how you steal votes." Manny chimed in.

"Are you willing to have an uncomfortable conversation?" Mrs. Obama asked Michigan, "Are you willing to..."

"DO SOMETHING!" They responded louder than they were the first time.

POTUS 2024: BALANCE THE SCALE

"Michigan... Let's give Kamala everything we've got. The next President of the United States of America—"

The audience cheered so loud; they drowned out Mrs. Obama's next choice of words. Madam Vice President, Kamala Harris received a booming, two-minute standing ovation as First Lady Obama walked with her to wave at the crowd from the stage.

Once she got started, Michigan made her feel right at home. "I know you want to say Kamalazoo, I heard you!" She joked with the front row which made the whole event center laugh, cheer, scream, and whistle.

"What an ice breaker," Isaac admitted.

"We've got that out of the way. OK." They all laughed again as she brought down the house leaving people feeling optimistic about the country's future with or without Booker's administration holding the reins.

One day was the last thing holding Booker back from the podium. He went to sleep confident in himself that night. He wrote and refined his first speech tens of times and practiced it ten times that. The preparation stage was over it was time to execute.

Thinking with experience, Booker was half dressed in yet another black suit. He held his shirt, tie, and blazer in a garment bag. With an hour to himself before heading across state, Booker called his father to do something he'd never done before.

Ring

"Hello?"

"Hey Pop."

"What's up, Mr. Garvey?"

"I'm headed that way in a little bit. Jazz n'them are coming to get me in a little bit."

"That's a fine woman."

Booker laughed, picking up where he left off. "I'm giving my first speech a little later. We're headed that way in about an hour. I'll text the group chat when I find out where."

"Check."

"I really called to say something I never said before, Pop because usually you're the one saying it… I told you." Booker shrugged, having a rare moment. "I told you, Pop. I'm running for president!" Booker was smiling.

"Yea…" Garvey admitted, quickly. "Yea, you told me. I just try to keep you grounded, Trip. You're doing big things. It's easy to lose yourself if nobody challenges you by fear of reality.

"Most people see life how it is and adapt to get ahead. Visionaries adapt but while doing so, they end up creating their own reality. That's you, Trip. POTUS 2024, I'm Booker Garvey II and I approve this message."

A two-hour trip across state came with an update as they reached city limits. "We're headed over to Hastings Street. They've built a stage inside a big outdoor tent where the old Castle Theatre used to be. You'll be speaking to Detroit's top activists, activist organizations, community leaders, public safety officers and their superiors.

"It holds about one hundred fifty people so don't expect Lions tailgate numbers or anything close to it. This is an intimate event that we've been invited to speak at as representatives of the Realist Critical Thinking Party. We've granted exclusive rights to the LOTT News Network to cover the campaign in order to properly control the narrative," Isaac added to keep Booker up to speed.

"News stations won't know what happened until we tell them. If this was business, think of it as a direct-to-consumer relationship. No need in spending millions and even billions on advertisements. We know where the money is."

"We just have to direct it towards the RCTP," Jasmine said, while Isaac continued.

"LOTT Network's viewership has a lot of heavy hitters. This is your second opportunity to gain some kind of motion in the RCTP's PAC." Isaac finished their conversation as they took a seat.

"That was a lot. But I'm ready for whatever. What time does it start?" Booker asked.

"Thirty minutes," Jasmine answered, nonchalantly.

"Aw shit." Booker started stretching, cracking his neck, and straightening his posture. He was starting to get himself mentally prepared.

Jasmine shrugged saying, "Your political career officially started the second you entered the Sprinter on Thursday, October 24, 2024. You still ready for whatever?" Jasmine asked, reminding him of his own words.

"I am. But thirty minutes? Got damn! I thought we'd have a little down time first."

"You'll be fine. You just had a damn good warm up Thursday and a visual of excellence yesterday," Isaac said, in an encouraging tone of voice.

"Unlike Thursday, when you get out of the Sprinter, you'll need to be dressed and ready to deliver. As soon as we walk in, they're going to wrap up their address. Let the people know why you're there. Introduce you then it's all on you after that." Jasmine gave Booker an overview of the night ahead of them. There was nothing more to do except finish the drive across town.

The area transformed greatly in the nighttime. There were lights and candles illuminating the white carpet runway. A large pond had been upgraded to support a waterfall. Its mist helped water the white rose garden next to it. All of which made up the front area that had been converted to a courtyard for socializing.

"Damn, this looks exquisite," Booker said as they arrived.

"This is the annual Street-Police Fundraiser and Banquet. They usually raise anywhere between $10k to $50K plus. One year they raised a million dollars. Sometimes they allocate it all to one cause. Sometimes it's split between multiple groups," Isaac informed him.

"They're consistent donors to the RCTP's candidates and you're the RCTP's first presidential candidate. So, you may get the lump sum if you play your cards right." Jasmine chimed in again.

"Well, it's time to play one of these aces I'm holding," Booker said with his chest puffed out.

"It's about…" Isaac paused to look Booker eye to eye. "It's about got damn time," he said. "That's the Booker Garvey III who needs to deliver that speech in five minutes. Questions?"

"Are we staying for dinner? I'm starving."

"We're in and out. Presidential candidates have things to do. We can get food on the way back to Kalamazoo," Jasmine answered.

"Alright, I'm ready when y'all are."

"Norman, it's go time." Isaac slowly nodded his head. Isaac hadn't shown much emotion the whole day, but it was clear to see that speeches for him was like gameday for a coach. Norman opened the door, as they exited one at a time with Booker coming out last. Norman closed the door behind them and drove off for the parking lot.

Walking down the runway, people in the courtyard entered the tent behind them. The greeter escorted the trifecta on stage, seated to the right of the speaker and without further ado, "The next President of the United States of America…"

Booker sat up straight as he ignored the beaded balls of sweat collecting on his forehead. "Booker… Garvey III!" The program's host shouted, introducing Booker to the crowd. A warm welcome was extended his way as he smiled, waving. Using the time to collect himself, a thumb swipe across his forehead like the blade of a windshield wiper went unnoticed.

Taking a page out of Manny's book, he greeted the crowd with a simple, "Good evening."

"Good evening!" They replied in strength.

Clearing his throat once more, he settled in at the podium with a few props and began his official presidential campaign announcement.

Since I was in 5th grade, I can recall having presidential aspirations. Why me? You may ask. I was born in a city that no longer has a public school district or a library… it still has citizens. Highland Parkers.

Booker's tone was very commanding from beginning to end. Isaac and Jasmine were smiling like proud parents watching it all from behind him. Jasmine crossed her fingers to stop from clapping and Isaac could only marvel with his hand on his chin.

"I'm also a writer. The greatest writer of my generation, greatest writer of my era, greatest writer of the 21st Century," Booker said with a natural pause before moving on to the next part of his speech.

A pretty, curvy, brown skin woman walked in mid speech and stole Booker's attention. In typical Booker Garvey III fashion, he eyed the woman to her seat. Winking at her before licking his lips, slyly. In the next second, he smoothly continued his speech as if it never happened.

If this is to be one nation under God, then we need to act like it because right now the devil's agents and non-believers are working hard as hell... We need to balance the scale. B GARV, POTUS 2024... out!

Booker saluted the audience, putting on a pair of black, Blenders Prime 21 sunglasses. Then picked up a copy of his first book, *Michigan International University* and shook the host's hand. The crowd showered the stage with their applause.

Waving from the front of the stage, he smiled publicly for the first time as an endorsed Politician. Booker felt like he had a shot again no matter how long it seemed.

Pumping his fist, Isaac was filled with energy as things unfolded in front of him. He and Jasmine nodded their heads at each other saying the same thing in unison.

"White House."

XIII: Headed West

"Alright this is the final stretch." Jasmine reminded Booker from the front room of the campaign office. Two days. Today and tomorrow. You have to give two speeches in two days, in two states, two time zones apart. I know better than to ask if you're ready by now." She stopped to look at Booker before asking, "How you feeling? Honestly."

"Tired. Hmmp." He admitted. "But I'll be alright. What are the polls looking like?"

Booker was handed a tablet. "Michigan has over ten million residents and almost three million have voted early. 46% Democrat, 43% Republican, 11% Third Party." Monica summarized from across the table.

"Thanks," Booker said, reading the results state by state. "Seven million people is a lot of people to account for."

"Close. Almost eight and a half million are registered with a little over seven million being active voters."

"That's still a lot of votes on the table. I see Isaac is over there looking at the map again. I'ma guess that means we're back on the road."

"Good guess." Monica nodded towards Isaac who was getting ready to speak.

"There's a Teachers' Union E-Board meeting across the street from where we'll be for your next speech. We've invited them to come over to hear your next speech… tonight."

"Tonight?" Booker asked. "Y'all are full of surprises. Boy, I tell you." Booker laughed. "I haven't even proofed it yet."

"Booker, it's been a week. You can't keep delivering the same speech. We're already behind. Didn't you just see the polls?" Lenice reminded him.

"She's right you've given that speech what twenty times?" Jasmine asked half serious.

"Twenty-six," he said with a self-induced cough in his elbow.

"That was so fake." Lenice looked disgusted, then took a bite of her bagel.

"Yeaaaah," he dragged out. "I mean yeah, you're right. It's time for something new. What time is tonight's speech?"

"9:00PM. You have a little more than twelve hours."

"That's not too bad."

"Alright, let's hear what you got," Lenice requested.

Booker stood up straight and began clearing his throat.

Good afternoon. Before we get started, I want to clear up some misconceptions about my campaign announcement.

"Nope, no you don't." Jasmine interrupted. "Not the time," she concluded, eating an egg patty with turkey sausage, cheese, and bell peppers.

"Damn, alright. Well, I'll be back. That's most of my introduction."

"Just remember these are our last thirty-six hours or so. We're at the point where everything counts. We only need to hear things that matter, right now. We'll clear up misconceptions and allegations later on all at once if at all," Isaac added, still studying locations on the map. "And it's Good evening, not good afternoon."

"Check!" Booker replied.

"Just remove the intro and give us what ya got so far," Jasmine requested. "I'm curious."

"Alriiight," Booker answered, stretching out the word.

Firstly, I'm only going to say this once. I'm not talking to my students right now. My students can't vote. I'm talking to their parents, guardians, their peers, elders, and anyone else over the age of eighteen and is registered to vote!

"The *anyone older than eighteen* line is cool, but we'll address that later on too unless you find a better way to word it," Jasmine added. "Continue."

"OK." Booker added notes to his notebook, licking the corners of his mouth as he jotted. *Two! Yes, I'm a LOTT Writer but at the moment, I'm writing a book in life. Right now, in front of you. POTUS 2024, July 5th is the day we balance the scale in literature as well!*

I just want to be clear. At this point, this is bigger than me. This is not an independent thing anymore. This was an independent thing when you saw me at Hart Plaza with my megaphone before April's draft in Downtown Detroit. This was an independent thing when I was the King of the Hill in Grand Rapids. Now, I am the presidential candidate for the Realist Critical Thinking Party.

"Cut it. Eight point two-five second attention spans, Mr. Garvey. Get-to-the-point." Isaac reminded him one word at a time.

Adding more notes to his notepad, he continued his speech.

"OK, so this is the new beginning," he said, requesting a fresh listen.

Good evening,

We're going to get real today. And a hit dog might holla. So if you take heed to what I say and feel emotional about it, shame on you in the first place.

Today, we are here to talk about something that affects a growing number of 347,337,793 people, roughly ⅓ of all American citizens. That group includes rough estimates of 3.8 million teachers, 49.6 million students and 63.1 million parents with children under eighteen.

We're going to start this scenario in high school. I'm a prolific writer but this is nothing but facts. It really happened. 2005. In the 313 Highland Park, Detroit.

Straight out of high school, I recruited some friends to start college with. I asked at least ten people and only one wanted to. I mean, he really wanted to go but couldn't because he was taking care of himself, and we graduated at seventeen. Which means he didn't qualify for financial aid as an adult. That's just the introduction. That isn't even the topic at hand. School Dream deferred count so far: one.

"What's the point of this?" Jasmine asked.

"Uhhh, pointing out a flawed system?"

"Save it. Use it somewhere else."

Booker added more notes, *I started as a business major before getting into education and I teach Math. So I'm good with numbers. So good, I can tell a story with numbers too. I'm a griot at the highest level.*

The journey started in 2005, I switched majors in 2007 and graduated college the first time in 2012. After graduation, my salary was $36,100. People I went to school with in Education called me lucky.

"OK, I'm lost now," Jasmine laughed. What is this speech about?"

"Teacher pay?" Booker questioned.

"You asking me? OK, fix what you need to, and we'll go over it again."

POTUS 2024: BALANCE THE SCALE

"OK." Booker shook his head, walking to the back of the store front office where he'd later emerge with a finished speech.

"Stay on task, Book!" Monica laughed, watching Booker go through the motions.

"OK!" After fifteen minutes of editing, he returned. Ready to deliver.

Good evening,

My fellow Americans, Today's topic we are going to talk about an issue that roughly ⅓ of the entire US population is facing. We're talking about approximately 347,337,793 Americans. That group includes about 3.8 million teachers, almost fifty million students and over sixty-three million parents with students under the age of eighteen.

The journey started in 2005, I switched majors in 2007 and graduated college the first time in 2012. After graduation, my salary was $36,100. People I went to school with in the field of Education called me lucky. Why? Some started out making 30k getting paid once a month.

I sidetracked my youth and matured quickly to be a leader and role model at twenty-four. I accepted that. I also accepted graduating 84k in debt because I wanted to better myself. You may wonder, well... why are you still there? Somebody had to go through it to tell you what's going on. I have never once heard a politician fight for teacher Pay well, you have. Me!

I made that sacrifice for children I don't know for families I never met. For what? What is my job description? In short, teach curriculum and citizenship. But what's expected of me? How much time you got?

Advisor, secretary, receptionist, liaison, doctor, nurse, counselor, camp counselor, bi-linguist, tri-linguist, lawyer, judge, jury, role model, mother/father figure, principal, mentor, coach, behavior specialist, welfare officer, food bank, mediator, referee, advocate, etc. etc.

All that is fine. It is what it is but pay us for it! We need to balance the scale! About a month ago, I was asked what teachers do on weekends. If we're lucky, we get to unwind and make it out Friday. Saturday in a building with strong chemistry may have a gathering at someone's house. Lesson plans on Sunday then back at it Monday morning. He said, "So, y'all only get one day off?" I thought, we are salary... we only get one day off. All of that to make $36,100 my first year.

That was 2013. This past fall, we negotiated new contracts where we received a 2.5% raise. At my salary, we're talking about, $1,625 or $62.50 every two weeks. My taxes and deductions are about 38-40%. So that 2.5% raise is about $38.75 every two weeks.

For what? What's my job description? To educate the leaders of tomorrow, today! We need to balance the scale!

My first year, I made $36,100. New teachers today in 2024, have second jobs, many of them. Just to survive. That's why I started writing ten years ago.

I got lucky to find a way to monetize my words. Some teachers come to work starving and have to put on a good face in front of twenty-five students, some of which are also starving... That's not right. That's wrong. What it's really doing is taking advantage of a teacher's loving nature.

If we really care about students, pay the teachers! Not only will you have happier teachers, but you'll get the best minds out there in front of our children. Brilliant minds want to be paid like it.

I turned down a teaching job in Dubai in 2015 because I was coming off a rough year with low scores and didn't want to leave like that because I had a reputation to maintain. They would've happily matched my salary because I was scheduled to get a raise that year. Their benefits are a little different though. It was tax free, free rent, included transportation to work and for leisure, two round trip tickets to the United States. Free healthcare too.

While in America, our highest paid teachers are million-dollar coaches because our country prioritizes sports and entertainment over its education system. They're teaching sports but they're teaching! I love to have fun too but at some point, we have to grow up, take control of things and balance the scale!

When elected president, teacher pay will either rise substantially and or teachers will be tax exempt. There is no way! And I mean no way! That our teachers should be working two jobs... we already have twenty plus, with half of them starting before we teach our first lesson...

We have a lot to talk about with the outdated, underappreciated education system in our country. We will decrease school and workdays by at least two hours for children and three hours for adults. Which means teachers get paid an extra hour for every day of the school year. We must treat our teachers better in this country.

With this new workday, the new full-time worker will qualify at twenty-five hours per week which means pay bumps are coming to offset the shorter day. What the pandemic taught us on the business side of things is that we can do more with less. Quality over quantity.

We're doing this so that families can spend more time with each other during daylight hours and won't need to use a sick day to take their child to their two o'clock appointment. Another reason for doing so is to keep our inner city high school students off the streets!

POTUS 2024: BALANCE THE SCALE

If full time used to be forty hours, we expect the remaining fifteen hours to go to our high school students so they have no reason not to have good grades for college and a nice checking account after graduation with a fast tracked savings. Hopefully with good interest rates.

If Henry Ford started the forty-hour work week at Ford Motor Company right here in Highland Park in 1922, then it only makes sense for someone from Highland Park to balance the scale one hundred two years later. POTUS 2024. B Garv... out!

The campaign office was quiet. Everyone stood still, nodding their heads. Thinking of what to say next. "That was personal," Jasmine said first.

"Very personal. I liked it. Truth hurts," Isaac added.

"I liked it too," Jasmine said.

"Good job, Book!" Monica cheered on, clapping. "You're getting good at this political thing." She pointed from her seat.

"Thanks, Monica. Y'all liked it for real?"

"Like I said, it was pretty personal. But personal information is needed for topics like this," Isaac replied.

"Aight, there it is. What time is the speech?" Booker asked.

"Their meeting is scheduled from 7:00-8:30. Our doors open at 8:30 and the program starts at 9:00." Lenice read notes from her iPad.

"Program?" Booker asked, clueless of what was going on.

"They really don't tell you anything. Y'all gotta stop doing that." Lenice laughed long and hard. "He's not green anymore. He's been on the road now.

"The RCTP is hosting a 1st Annual Voters Registration Party. Anyone with voter registration cards gets a gift bag with $50 gas cards. Booker bumper stickers. Booker T-shirts, and limited edition, Booker bobble heads," she said, bouncing the figure's head against gravity. "Those only go to the first one hundred people. fifty are presidential themed and fifty are teacher themed. We're expecting no more than five hundred people.

"It'll be pizza for anyone hungry and people will be able to register if they're not. They'll also get a bag. It won't have as much. Some candy and a $50 gas card. That's better than nothing." Lenice shrugged. "I think that sums it all up."

"There it is. Well do y'all need anything from me between now and then," Booker asked, making his way towards the door.

"Where you headed, Book?" Lenice asked.

"Ay, I'm at where I'm at and I'll be where I'll be." He saluted them on the way out.

"You talk too much, Niecy," said a silent observer.

"Uh oh. Claudine has the floor now," Isaac said, smirking. Instigating from the sideline.

"When have we ever told anybody, everything?" Claudine asked directly.

"Yeah, but those cases were different. We're usually with a candidate from the roota to the toota. We just picked him up last week!" Lenice said with some intensity. "Wait until he finds out the real bombshell."

"She's right." Monica confirmed, fixing the hair behind her ear.

"Even if she is, we can't look divided like that. Ever." Claudine replied. "And I think you got him ready for it."

"No. A surprise voters registration party is small compared to what's coming and you see how he responded to this," Lenice explained.

"Because you got him ready for it. He was on defense."

"How, Claudine?" Lenice asked, confused by it all.

"When you said, *They really don't tell you anything. Y'all need to stop that*, remember?" Claudine asked, leaning forward towards Lenice.

Monica didn't say a word, but the sound she made was more than enough, "Mmm."

Isaac and Jasmine looked at each other, raising their eyebrows. "Yeah. I remember. I probably didn't need to say that. But it should make the news coming in a few days a little easier to deal with having trust issues." Lenice laughed gingerly.

Isaac leaned back in his seat, locking his fingers behind his head. Closing his eyes, he hoped she was right.

Walking into the store front with good news that preceded her arrival, "I just met a guy at the bank who rents dunk tanks and money booths. I was able to get them both 25% off for the speech tonight."

Hanging up her jacket, she continued. "Annnd, he knows a company that can light up designs on the tent!" Julene was joyful. Turning around to see the mood of the room didn't match her own. "What happened in here? And where's Booker?" She asked. "You didn't tell him yet, did you?"

Far from there, Booker needed to balance his own scale. *It took me ten years just to get here. Ain't nobody give me shit. Why would I complain? Remember getting nothing, watching em cop them chains…*

Booker rapped along with his windows down, as the music banged off of the subwoofers of his speaker box. He was well across town not thinking of anything except the one thing he'd abandoned the entire duration of his campaign.

Looking through the window of the door, he walked in to try his luck. "Can I get a cart and I'm going nine holes today," he requested, handing the cashier his debit card.

"Alright and good morning to ya." She was high spirited.

"Good morning."

"Your total is $19.08."

Booker paid the cashier and walked to his trunk, removing his golf clubs and a few bottles of water. Loading them into the golf cart, Booker took off towards hole number one. The hole was one hundred eight yards away. Walking up to the teeing ground, Booker placed a blue golf ball on a tee and got comfortable with its placement while adjusting his swing.

Finding the sweet spot, he swung his pitching wedge, slamming the ball off the tee and onto the fairway, thirty yards in. An older man and two women the man's age approached the tee shortly after Booker drove towards the ball.

Trading clubs, he grabbed a gap wedge hoping for better results. Booker looked the part with his swing, but the contact wasn't landing at his desired angle. Four or five swings in, the old man drove up to Booker, asking, "You don't mind if we go ahead, do you?"

"No problem. Go ahead." Booker insisted. Picking up his phone, he sent a text message.

Lina Bina 😎
Today 10:07 AM

> I'm buns golfing when you're not here. I don't have anybody to show out in front of. This old man just asked to drive ahead I was so bad.

Delivered

Booker finally made it to the greens and on to the next hole where the old man and two ladies were finishing up on the fairway. Picking up his phone, he saw Lina texted him back.

Lina Bina 😊
Today 10:28 AM

> Poor baby. You know I'd be driving that cart! Vroooom!! 🚗

> LMAO! You def would. It's cool tho. I'm just warming up. I haven't golfed all year 😅
> Delivered

The old man and two ladies finished up at hole two and had just finished putting. The group began teeing off on the third hole as Booker did the same from one hundred thirteen yards out on hole number two.

Teeing a black ball this time, he hit it fifty-four yards off the tee. Then another forty yards off the fairway grounds. Trying his luck again with the pitching wedge, he was able to land onto the greens, finishing three over par.

Waiting on the group ahead, he made a call this time.

"Hello?" She answered.

"How you be?" He asked.

"Gooood. How are you?"

"Even better now."

"Awww."

"I'm waiting on them now that I'm warmed up. Would it be petty if I rode up to them and asked if I could pass them?"

"Uhn unn don't." She giggled. "Please don't."

Booker's next hole was a straight away. While the group ahead was on a C-Shaped hole that ended near Booker's tee off spot. Booker paused his call when he realized he'd been absent for too long. The old man was trying to get his attention.

"You're not supposed to be driving on the greens," he said.

"Alright, man. Sorry," Booker said, holding his hand up.

"You love talking in movie quotes." Lina laughed. "You probably got yo hand up too."

"Yup and you know what's next," Booker said.

"Mr. President, don't."

"I can't believe you just said that." Booker laughed. "So that's how you gon talk me down now, huh?"

"Yup. Now get off the greens." Lina joked and laughed again.

POTUS 2024: BALANCE THE SCALE

"It's smooth," he said, driving up a few feet to the tee ground.

The old man smiled and waved while the second of the group took a swing with her putter. "I'm about to FaceTime you. I'm warmed up and need to stunt on this old man, aight?"

"You are *so* silly. OK."

The phone rang on Lina's end to answer as a FaceTime call and she did so. "Heyyyy stranger!" She waved. "Long time no seeeee." She sang, holding a note.

"It ain't been that long." Booker squeezed his face in disapproval.

"It's been long enough. We'll talk about that later. Go ahead, Tiger."

Booker grabbed a seven iron for the one hundred twenty-five-yard distance to the hole. Standing shoulder width apart, he adjusted his swing and whiffed. The club went over the top of the ball, missing it all together.

"That was just practice." Lina laughed.

"There it is."

Approaching the tee again, he lined up the club with the ball and made a couple practice swings before striking and that time, he struck gold.

"Good shot!" Lina shouted, clapping.

"That looks like it's going in." He tracked the ball as it landed on the greens.

"Of course, it is!"

"It went in!" He shouted as it rolled into the bottom of the cup. "Let's gooooo!" Booker jumped into the air, swinging his fist.

"Good shot!" The old man pumped his fist at Booker.

Booker finished the rounds before heading home to shower and rest up before the big speech.

He ignored so many messages from The Party, he forgot they even texted him. Reaching for his phone, he sat on the couch as he put on a shirt and dried his hair. Tossing the towel across his shoulders, he caught up in the group chat.

The Party
Today 5:00 PM

Jazz
> We need you ready at 6 and it's already 5. Please be on time, Booker.

Isaac (NJ7.1)
> He knows

Lenice
Does he?
Too soon?
MRS! Monica
Way too soon
Claudine
Jazz
We'll be there at 6, Booker.

Having been caught up to speed, he walked to the closet to figure out what to wear. Seeing black and blue golf balls on the dresser and his navy blue sweatpants on the floor. His choice was made for him. Reaching for a blue dress shirt, he grabbed a blue, corduroy blazer and a two-toned blue tie.

For his lower body he chose black slacks and a pair of black, Playoff 8 Air Jordan gym shoes. Putting his shirt, tie, and jacket back on a hanger, he watched some pregame football coverage until Norman arrived with the Sprinter.

Ring

"Yooo!" Booker greeted.

"What's good, Mr. President. It's the day before Election Day AND you bout to drop a dawg ass speech tonight. How you feel, brodie?"

Booker laughed hearing what he'd been up to from someone else. "I'm good dawg. I feel great. Got some golfing in earlier. Hit my first hole in one! Shit was crazy dawg."

"I already know you hit your first hole in one." Manny laughed. "Yo rap name is Miracle. What else are you supposed to be doing on the day of your new speech, the day before Election Day?"

"You ain't lying." Booker laughed at the truth.

"How you feeling about the speech? The first one gon be hard to follow up."

"Honestly bro, I've been waiting my whole life to say what I'm about to say tonight and my speech tomorrow."

"Yeah, you always have been an ol, Booker T. Tupac Malcolm Martin Luther Louis Marvin Garvey Seale Newton Sam Cooke Muhammad Ali King Jr. ass muh fucka."

"Mannn, what!? That's the second time I dun heard some shit like that." Booker laughed, not knowing where to start.

"For real bro. You're always fighting for teachers to get paid or for broke ass schools to get money like they do in the burbs; or speaking up for your students, their families n'shit like that. Like you said…" Manny paused to bring his point home with the right words. "You been waiting on this shit yo whole life. You got this shit dawg."

"My man! I appreciate that, dawg. For real."

"You know it. What time you leaving?"

"Norman's ass will be here in five minutes or less, dawg. Guaranteed. If not him, *somebody* will be here in five minutes or less."

"Punctual then a muh fucka they are. Claudine be hit'n me up a day early for shit that's due in two days."

Booker laughed. "Sounds about right. That's because Julene be on all they head. She's really the mutha fucka."

"She reminds me of Claire Huxtable." Manny joked.

"For real. I said the same shit."

Beep.

"Hold on dawg," Booker got a text from Norman saying he'd arrived.

"What I tell you." Booker laughed again. "5:55. Norman said he's outside and if I don't come, they gon call at six on the nose. Usually, I'll walk out now but I'ma head down *at* six. They think I'm mad because they don't tell me shit till the last minute and Lenice called them out on it."

"Word? That's what they was talmbout in the chat?"

"Yeah," Booker chuckled. "I don't give a fuck." He laughed. "Me and you came up with shit on the fly. I don't give a fuck what they got planned as long as the shit works. I needed a break today though and they gave me a reason." Booker shrugged. "They was gon have me in that muh fucka rehearsing and rewriting all day; I already know how it was going down. I've read it enough times. I'm saying it how I practiced but I'ma let it bleed too so it might come out a little different."

"That's real. Ay, I can't wait to hear it. They're giving me the front-center camera tonight. I'ma use the 7500 for this one. Let's see what the hype is about."

"Good shit. The 7500 is a badd muh fucka I just wish it had the door on the back like the 5300. Ay I gotta roll, mane. It's 5:57. I guess I'll go out there now."

"Fasho. I'll see y'all when y'all get here. Good luck."

"Bet. Good look, bro."

Booker hung up the phone and took the private penthouse elevator closest to the parking lot to save time. Walking in a steady stride, he reached the Sprinter at 6:00:49PM.

Norman and Booker shook hands before Norman took his bags. He opened the door to awkward behavior as Booker broke the ice. "Boyyyy, y'all clean up better than a janitor! Damn, y'all look good," he said as everyone smiled and laughed. "I stole that line from Manny."

Climbing into the vehicle, he hugged them all on his way to the bench. "A day and a half, y'all. Y'all ready?" He asked.

"I don't have to give the speech. Of course, I'm ready. Ready to hear it." Monica laughed high fiving Jasmine and Claudine.

"Well, I'm ready and you look wonderful, Booker. I'm glad you're in great spirits. It's going to be a great time tonight." Julene put her hand on his thigh as she spoke.

"Thanks, Mrs. J. I can't wait. Let's do this!"

"Hey, Booker?" Jasmine felt the patch on the elbow of Booker's blazer. "This is nice…"

"Thanks, Jazz." Booker smiled. "With those cool ass earrings you got on." He lightly cuffed her dangling metal.

"Stop." She blushed over her rose gold makeup, still feeling the material as they resumed their conversation. "We tried to bring out your Soror when we started organizing but she's out of the country."

"My Soror? A Zeta? Who?" He asked questions in threes.

"The Mayor, Booker. You of all people should know this."

During their two-hour drive to Highland Park for his final Michigan address, no one brought up what happened earlier in the day; where he was, or anything about his speech. They just enjoyed the moment knowing their journey together would soon reach a split road.

Reaching their destination, Norman slowed to a halt at the original, Henry Ford Motor Company assembly plant. It was opposite to the meeting hall. The factory had been long abandoned, but the RCTP was able to rent the parking lot to host their activity inside a large sphere, dome tent designed to host five hundred people.

POTUS 2024: BALANCE THE SCALE

The entire dome had been lit up like an American flag with rotating stars. "I know I'm supposed to act like I've been here. But those twinkling stars are cool as shit."

Exiting the vehicle, they walked into the venue at 8:11PM. Ensuring everything was still in place, they made their way to the waiting area just before the doors opened. "Alright, Booker. We're out of here." Isaac announced. "We'll be back to get you at five minutes to."

Alone with just his thoughts, the door opened with a *knock, knock, knock!* As Monica brought him five bottled waters, a sweat rag, and a portable speaker. "Good luck, Book," she said. Leaving as quickly as she arrived.

"Thanks."

Going over his speech once more, he zoned out listening to 1990s Soul music to mellow out. "Giving you the best that I've got... baybeeeh." He sang offkey as another, *knock, knock, knock!* On the door preceded its visitors. "Five minutes, you ready?" Jasmine asked.

"I was until you just said that. Now, I got the bubble guts."

"T-M-I," Jasmine responded as they left the room, disgusted by his admission.

Booker stayed back to flatulate, closing the door behind him. Tying shoes that didn't need to be, he was able to stall while the air cleared.

Reaching the group, they led him to the stage area where he hugged everyone one last time before separating. "Our table is one o'clock to the podium. Good luck, Booker." Isaac said as they departed.

Booker stayed backstage, listening to the host. The dome was set up so that the first room seated groups of twenty in a semicircle around the stage. The activities and food tables were curtained off behind the stage.

"I know it's already nine but immediately after the speech, there will be a meet and greet. Then Game Time sponsored by Lucky McWallace and the folks at the ShowTime Center. Dinner is right after at 10:30PM."

Ready to be called, Booker went over his lines until it was time. About five minutes later, he could hear the transition was being made towards his introduction.

"You may know some of his work, especially if you read LOTT Magazine. You've probably read Wake Up Little Lion to your children. And I *know* you read Prize Fighter, Bad Move, and Nobody Cares from the Tyme series like I have. Set right here in Highland Park!

"He's a twelve-year veteran teacher, a Master of Education Administration. Michigan's first president since Gerald Ford. Yeah, I said it... HP's Finest, Booker! Garvey! The Thirrrrd!"

Booker walked up to the podium, saluting the crowd, holding more props. He shook the hosts' hand and as the crowd settled, he got straight to business with his disclaimer.

Good evening,

My fellow Americans, today we're going to get real, and a hit dog might holla. So if you take heed to anything I say and get emotional about it, shame on you in the first place.

The crowd laughed as he banged the podium, prompting him to look away or else he might have joined them. Throughout his speech, Booker held the audience's attention for eight minutes of pure passion.

You may wonder, 'Well, why are you still going through it?' Because somebody had to go through it to let you know what's going on.

Booker was on a roll, heads nodded like a concert with various sounds of agreement. "Go ahead!" One man shouted.

We're doing this so that high school students can stay out of the streets. The forty hours that their parents used to spend at work, now down to twenty-five. We expect those fifteen to go to their students. If Henry Ford ushered in a forty-hour work week, right here in Highland Park. Then I guess it's up to a Highland Park kid to balance the scale. POTUS 2024, B GARV... out!

Booker put on a pair of blue Ray Ban sunglasses. Picked up his book, *Wake Up Little Lion* and left the stage shaking his brother Ian's hand.

"You did that!" Ian shouted with excitement.

"My man!" Booker smiled.

Walking towards the front of the stage, the crowd let him have it. The cheers were so loud, all he could do was smile and say, "Thank you!"

Exiting the stage left, the crew was back together to embrace Booker once again, showering him with support. "The only bad thing about that speech is giving it again knowing you'll never top *that*!" Isaac was shaking Booker's hand vigorously. The smiles were gone. He was intense.

The host prompted the directors to raise the curtains while he gave them a breakdown of the night's events. "Alright, y'all! We have dunk tanks, money booths, Pop a Shots, Football throws, mini golf, laser tag, and all kinds of other stuff.

"Booker Garvey III will be out soon for the meet and greet. Dinner is at 10:30PM right here in this same spot. But only if you're registered to vote! You saw the invitation. If you have your voter's registration card to the right, if you need to register… to the left, to the left."

The crowd did what they needed to while Booker lived in the moment. After wiping the sweat from his forehead, he put the cloth back in his inner pocket. Then they went back out for the meet and greet. The crowd applauded again as they surrounded Booker for pictures and autographs while Manny captured every minute.

As things simmered down, Booker became one with the people. It was also time to have a conversation that was much needed to get a pulse of the streets. "What's good, brodie?" Booker slapped hands with his brother, Ian.

"You got it, my man. Good shit, again."

"Good look. Good look." Booker repeated. "I see the streets came out for this one. I saw TJ, his Pops, and the Money Men." Booker realized, looking around. "I just got done talking to Stan, Victor and a few of my dawgs who played for the Jets with me way back when too."

"Yeah, you did that!" Ian nodded his head, pounding fists. "Between me, you, and sis, we went to school with half the city. It's like a mini class reunion in this muh fucka."

"Who's that with you tho? Thickums and the short, dark-skinned cutie?" Ian asked for himself.

"Mannnn, thicka than a Snicker. She's super married tho."

"Super married?"

"Yeah, she told me three times in one sentence." Booker shook his head.

Ian laughed before Booker told him, "That's Monica. Claudine is the other one. Y'all around the same age too. She was born in seventy-eight."

"Aw, that ain't shit but three years."

"We're all grown-grown after thirty." Booker agreed.

Entering the wee hours of the morning, the event ended at midnight. Taking off for the West Coast in the morning, their next stop was Downtown to the Renaissance Center to check into their hotel rooms for the night. Norman loaded the buggy with their luggage as they arrived while Monica handled lodging.

The penthouse had eight bedrooms, eight bathrooms, a dining area, and kitchen. There was a full sized living room; where they conversed about and talked over the early voting projections playing on the TV. Isaac, Jasmine, Julene, and Norman were the first to call it a night. It was just before 2:00AM.

"Alright, y'all. I'm old and sleepy. The plane takes off at 9:30AM. Breakfast is at six. We're leaving at eight o'clock. With or without you. That's to everyone but Booker. Goodniiiiiight," Jasmine told them with a big wink and matching sound effect.

"Everyone but Booker, huh? That's wrong." Monica joked.

"The rest of us can be replaced at this point," Claudine confirmed.

"Tell em, Jazz! Y'all better be ready by 8AM. That's all *we* know." Booker and Manny laughed, slapping hands.

"You see them?" Monica pointed.

"Wrong." Claudine confirmed.

The group continued to get smaller as time went on. "Well, goodnight y'all." Claudine waved. "He's already asleep." She pointed at Manny, walking towards the hall.

"I'm right behind you, girl. Wait for me," Monica said without moving a muscle. "I'm so proud of you, Booker. You've grown so much." She yawned as her sleepy eyes watered a tad.

"Thanks, Monica. I appreciate that."

"One more day. Goodnight." She reminded him. Standing to her feet, she slid her slippers across the floor with quick steps to catch up to Claudine.

POTUS 2024: BALANCE THE SCALE

"Yupper, one more day. Gooood-night!"

Booker tried waking Manny up before calling it a night, but he wouldn't budge. Leaving him where he rested, Booker got some shut eye before his tour continued in the morning.

Traveling the next day in a pair of khaki-colored slacks instead of sweats, Booker had an idea. "Jazz," Booker called from the living room, finishing his breakfast.

"What's up, Book?" She responded.

"Can we make a stop before the airport?"

"How long you need?"

"Thirty minutes."

"Let's say an hour. We'd have to leave by seven," she reasoned.

"Aight, y'all," Booker announced. "We gotta get outta here by seven. Change of plans."

"Everybody's ready but you, brother." Isaac broke the news swiftly.

After the show got on the road, The Party exited the freeway. A few turns later, there was a large Pistons basketball where Norman would soon turn left. Then another left shortly after, taking them to a dead-end street. "There it is," Booker pointed to a house at the end of the block.

"That's Meech and T old crib, ain't it?" Manny asked.

"Yepper! This is where we're shooting our PSA."

Booker got with Manny to describe the look he wanted for the video. Setting up the tripod, Manny was ready to roll and would even make a cameo.

Booker put on his shirt, tie, and blazer then walked slowly towards the camera and pointed to the house behind him delivering a powerful public service announcement for all of America's citizens.

As a forgotten soul in the classroom, I know what it feels like to be overlooked. The people who grew up in the house behind me were overlooked by the penal system, the justice system and society. They were celebrated in the Hip Hop community.

Demetrius "Big Meech" Flenory and his brother Terry "Southwest T" Flenory created a quarter to a half billion-dollar enterprise on the inland of the United States from the late 1980s to the 2000s. What's the problem? It was drug money. That might scare you away but not me. I'm a teacher and teachers don't quit on our students, the same way I won't quit on our citizens.

Booker began undoing his tie as soon as he finished. "The man is on fire!" Isaac shouted out of character, fanning Booker with the papers he held as they got back on the road. "Next stop, Oakland California!"

Arriving at the airport with time to spare as it wasn't yet 9AM. They were able to take the employee entrance to access the airport's private hangar. Scanning his ID card, Norman bypassed security. Approaching the private jet that awaited them on the runway, an earlier flight would be readily available. Booker's eyes bulged as he felt a bump next to him. It was Jasmine, shaking her head no.

Exiting the Sprinter, they boarded the private jet being greeted individually by the flight attendants. Taking a seat, Booker's sunglasses effectively hid his eyes. They were dancing all over the place absorbing what they saw.

The jet was big enough for twenty people and had more than enough room for the current party. The middle section's seats had been removed to create a lounge area for its passengers. Booker wasn't the biggest fan of air travel and preferred to sleep during that time.

Awaking as they landed, Booker stretched his legs and stood up ready to get off the plane. But first he needed some water. Making his exit, he stopped by the refreshment stand, grabbed a few bottled waters and some snacks for the road.

Walking down the stairs, he walked arm in arm with Jasmine, so she didn't fall in her high heels. "We've got a busy day today, Booker," she informed him. "It's… 10:05. We're only here for a hot second. You'll be speaking at 11:00AM across the street from Merritt College here in Oakland. Then we're right back on a plane to Kalamazoo no later than noon to vote. Is that too much?"

"This is it, Jazz. So, whatever it takes."

"That's what I like to hear, darling," she said with a side hug. Jasmine kissed Booker's cheek then wiped away her lipstick.

Reaching ground level, Booker and Jasmine walked and talked to the Sprinter. "Did I ever tell you I had a student named Jasmine earlier this year? In the class that left in June."

Jasmine gasped. "Nooo, you did *not*."

"I promise you. When I write, I try not to use names of anybody I know. And with *every* book that I've written, a student pops up in my class with the same name as a character from that book. Even my first live book, POTUS 2024. This time it was lil Jasmine and Jasmine Clarke."

"That is so precious." Jasmine said. Unhooking arms to reach inside her oversized purse, "Here, give her this." Jasmine removed a golden case with a matching pen that she unboxed. "Can you read that?" She asked, handing him the case.

"Jasmine: A Gift From God," He read the pen, holding it sideways.

"That's what it means. Tell her I said to never forget that she's a gift."

"She's in middle school now." Booker replied disappointedly.

"Keep it anyway just in case you see her again."

"She might have to pry this from my fingers." Thoroughly examining the pen, "This is a nice ass pen and I love nice ass pens, Jazz. Besides... you're *my* gift from God." He smiled. "Believe that."

"Aw, Booker." She smiled back. Wrapping her arm around his waist sideways, she leaned her head on his arm saying, "Ok. If you don't see her again before packing up the class for the last time, consider it an early retirement gift. One of them."

"One of them." Booker laughed. "That's what I like to hear. Good deal." Unzipping his coat, he put the pen case inside his inner pocket as they headed to their destination.

After a twenty-minute drive, Booker could see the tent from afar. He knew exactly where they were headed. It had become their trademark. This time the tent was located right on Campus Drive and was twice the size as the last. Students were starting to make their way from campus, seeing the tent go up over the last twenty-four hours.

Entering through the east doors, The Party looked around seeing that everything was in place. Next, they located the resting area and dressing rooms.

"This is our last event. Everything else from here on out are guest appearances. Keep the ball rolling. Booker, you're doing a damn good job, man. Let's finish strong and make it a great job." Isaac praised Booker's rookie run.

"Yes sirrrrr!" Booker saluted Isaac.

"Right now, I won't lie to you. It's between Vice President Harris and President Trump. Third Parties are making a splash with some solid numbers over 13%," Isaac concluded.

"Damn."

"It's a long day, Booker Garvey III and we'll let you be. See you at 10:55 s-h-a-r-p." Isaac spelled out the letters, closing the door behind them.

"OK." Booker chuckled.

Booker reviewed his final speech a few times, pacing the floor when his concentration was snapped by the *Knock, knock, knock!* Sound on the door before it opened. "Here's your waters, sweat rag, and speaker." Monica handed Booker a small duffle bag. "Are you ready?"

"I am. I thought I'd be nervous like last night. Probably because that was home, and I won't ever see any of these people again in my life. But I'm good. I'm ready," he said.

"You look tired."

"I am." Booker admitted.

"I'll be right back."

Booker reached into the duffle bag, grabbed his towel, and walked over to the sink against the wall. Running hot and cold water on the towel, he covered his face with it in cycles. *Knock, knock, knock!* The door went and opened. "Here." Monica handed Booker an eyeglasses case.

"Damn, some Yays?" He asked, admiring the gold trim on the glasses.

"I think this is included in acting like you've been here." Monica laughed. "I understand though. This can be a lot for somebody our age. I've been working with the RCTP for seven elections in ten years and was an intern before that. So, I've seen it grow a lot." Monica admitted. "But this is all coming at you in less than a month."

"Who you telling? I feel like a C-list celebrity or some shit. But I can't act like one."

"Ooooh that must be sooo tough." Monica laughed. "You will be alright. I am so joking. You should be proud of yourself. I hope you are. This is a big deal."

"I will be later. Especially after tonight. I don't plan on doing anything political until after I drop the book on the 5th of July."

"Look, I get it. Just make sure to keep in touch," she said, grabbing Booker's hand.

"Monica… you're *Mrs.* Jarreau, right?" He asked.

"I am *not* married." Monica took her ring off and switched it to her right hand. "This is my grandmother's ring. I wear it to stop men from trying me so much."

"Damn…" Booker closed the distance between them. She took his towel and sat it on the table to hold his other hand.

"Monica, Baby." He leaned towards her. Hugging her body closely, Booker cuffed her glutes with both hands.

Monica's freshly manicured fingertips crossed behind Booker's neck, as she stared into his eyes. Meeting him halfway, they kissed and slid tongues.

Booker's hands were all over Monica's body and hers were making their way down his. Until she stopped to say, "Booker, we can't do this here. Especially not now." Then bit her lip, saying, "Damn, you sexy."

"Me? Shiiit, that's *you*." Booker insisted. "You don't know how bad I used to feel, hugging you," he said with his arms still wrapped around her.

Looking into her eyes, he said, "Before now at least." He smirked. "This feels good as a muh fucka. I love yo hugs. Yo body is so soft." Booker rubbed her butt while they conversed as she hung around his body.

"I knew it was something going on. It seemed like you were scared of me."

"Got damn, Monica. Why didn't you say something sooner?"

"We work *way* too close together." She dismissed the notion. "I don't know why I grabbed your hand, honestly. Probably because if I didn't, I might've never seen you again." Monica seemed to have internalized her words and appeared slightly saddened.

"I don't know if you're running again in 2028. None of us do until you sign the contract. I knew all of that before, but I never really thought about it until you said that about the audience."

"You coulda texted me."

"Why would I text you?" She asked quickly. "If you didn't text me, today could've been our last time seeing each other." She assured him with near certainty. "Well, I guess I would've seen you for your inauguration."

Booker paused, to say, "That's what I like to hear. But I fasho wouldn't have texted you. I just *knew* you were happily married."

"Everything happens for a reason, I guess?" She suggested.

Booker leaned in to kiss her again. Squeezing her sides inwards until she stopped him. Holding his belt buckle with one hand, pushing his chest away with the other, she said, "Booker, we have to stop. There's a Three-Knock Policy around here."

"Whatever you're doing, be able to wrap it up in three knocks. For stuff just like this. People can't come in and do business without feeling awkward because folks can't keep their lips to themselves." Monica kissed Booker at the end of her sentence.

"You need to do something about that." Her eyes went south, still holding onto his belt buckle. Biting her bottom lip, she tapped his pants. Slowly, she dragged her finger down the bulge of his slacks.

"Damn," she said, pulling her hand back as it jumped in response to her touch.

"I have to gooo." Monica grabbed his shirt to pull him closer. Laying her hand on his chest, she kissed him once more; rushing towards the door while Booker took a seat as it sounded.

Knock, knock, knock! Claudine walked in, looking at the two with side eyes. "Have you seen Manny?" She asked. Looking at Booker with a slight wrinkle between her eyebrows.

"Naw. He said he was going to pass out QR codes and interview people outside." Booker assured her.

"OK…" she said, slowly.

Monica walked out with Claudine while she stared at her without saying anything.

"What?" Monica asked.

"You tell me what?"

"Girl, nothing."

"Then why you look like that?"

"Like what?"

"Like, who shot John?"

"Girl, I ain't shoot nobody." Monica denied her claim.

"Yeah, you better not have."

Booker took some time to gather himself before he finished getting dressed. Finally having his head on straight, he was back to rehearsal.

Knock, knock, knock! Went the door opening. Alright, Booker. Five minutes!" Isaac said loudly, clapping his hands.

"I only need four," he replied, calmly.

"Good answer." Isaac patted him on the back.

Walking to the stage, Booker hugged everyone and quickly massaged Monica's back during their interaction. She made a small giggle in his ear that went unnoticed.

Making his way to the podium; for the first time in his political career, he had to wait for the audience's applause to stop. Waving to the crowd, he began his speech. "Good evening, my fellow Americans…"

"Good evening," they replied strongly. Booker paused briefly before continuing after an unexpected surprise.

"I would first like to start by thanking everybody who hopped on this journey with us. It's been a fun ride and if this is the last time that I see you, it was great meeting you," he said, immediately locking eyes with Monica.

Booker looked the opposite direction and back at her again as she blushed, looking down at the table. Claudine and Julene sat directly across from her. Julene smiled at her reaction, asking her sister, "Have you noticed those two have been acting different since we left Detroit?"

"Nope," Claudine answered confidentially. "I noticed this afternoon. Not long after we got here." She confirmed her suspicion, smirking.

"They'd be cute together." Julene whispered. "Monica's so supportive."

"Yeah, they would… until another woman walks by. You can't take Booker seriously." Claudine objected. "You know I like Booker. I love, Booker. I just don't want to see her get hurt. That's all."

"Maybe she's the one."

"Or two, three, four, five." Claudine laughed bumping Julene's arm that was posted on the table as they stopped gossiping to hear Booker's speech.

"We *will* rehabilitate the country's nonviolent felons, who displayed superior abilities." Booker took the microphone off its stand, impromptu. He got much more comfortable afterwards and started to loosen up. "We will tap into their minds and figure out why they did what they did. Which is usually because of poverty. Which means their government failed them."

"Look," Claudine said to Julene. Nodding at Monica, she was all in, holding her hands under her chin, smiling.

Jasmine heard their chatter that time and looked up as Claudine nodded. Putting two and two together, she whispered her findings to Isaac as he looked over and shrugged. "I'm surprised it took this long." He admitted.

"Yeah, me too." Jasmine concurred.

"Senate Race of 2000 was *very* handsy if you remember."

"Handsy?" She questioned. "The Three-Knock Policy came after it. Do I remember?" She repeated. "How could I forget?"

"Goo-Goo eyes are nothing major. A kiss, maybe. If that."

"What makes you think only a kiss?"

"Because they're in the, *Can't hide it if they tried*, stage. Those kinds of butterflies still have innocence to them." Isaac schooled her on body language.

"Yeah, for now." Jasmine laughed quietly as they listened to Booker wrap up his speech.

"Same with the gang bangers: Blood, Crips, Vice Lords, GDs, Latin Kings, all of them. We invite you to the Homeland Defense. Bang for our country or not at all." Booker said, waving off with his hand. "We believe in your strength and together, we can get back to your organization's original roots… to protect the communities from foreign invasion…"

Standing up to meet Booker backstage, The Party walked towards the front while Booker signed off. "POTUS 2024, B GARV… out!" Saluting for the first time on the West Coast, Booker put on a pair of gold, Blenders Prime 21 sunglasses. He picked up the book *Nobody Cares* and started shaking hands as soon as he left the podium.

    The audience stood, cheered, clapped, and whistled while Booker embraced it all a bit longer than usual. After almost a half-minute, he walked off stage, shaking hands with America's future.

    The country didn't seem too big to Booker anymore. Everywhere he went lately, he felt celebrated. He could only hope it all translated into votes at the end of the day.

XIV: Homecoming

Booker slept half the plane ride before feeling his body shake. Peeling open his eye lids, he peeked through them to see what was happening. Being surrounded by his elders of the council, he had to ask, "What's going on?"

"Booker." Isaac wasn't smiling. His face was unreadable. "We need to talk." His chest rose before his next set of words as he took a deep breath.

Knowing what it was about, Booker acted as if he didn't. "What's up?"

"Booker, we made a discovery a couple weeks ago, but we were in too deep to do anything about it. We actually tried and got denied unless there are extenuating circumstances that trigger a very specific situation. Which is still very possible and why we waited until now to even bring up. This is one of those *we'll cross that bridge when we get there,* type of situations. Well, we've reached the waters."

Booker sat up straight, no longer knowing what Isaac was talking about. Listening closely, he was already asking questions in his head. "There's no easy way to say it, so I'll be frank."

Booker took a deep breath himself waiting to hear what he knew was bad news. "Do you remember one of the first things we talked about?" Isaac asked.

"Uhhh," Booker thought aloud.

For time's sake, Isaac answered for him. "I told you we're winners, Booker and that we choose who to add to our roster without applicants."

"Oh, yeah. Definitely."

"This is harder than I thought it'd be." Isaac inhaled deeply. "Long story short, Booker. Your name won't be on the ballot."

POTUS 2024: BALANCE THE SCALE

Booker was instantly deflated with slouched shoulders. Wondering, "Why not?"

"You have to file paperwork naming your vice president and other information." Isaac handed Booker a piece of paper listing all of the requirements.

"They were to be submitted by August 30th. We started filing paperwork on your behalf Wednesday, October 23, 2024. We couldn't do anything officially until you joined the RCTP."

Booker didn't know what to think. All of his questions escaped the mind but one. "What now?" He asked, squeezing his forehead.

"Well, the very specific situation is for there to be a discrepancy in votes so great that they have to be accounted for," Isaac summarized.

"Huh?" Booker replied.

"In layman's terms, you'll have to be written in on the ballots. Even still, the votes won't be counted unless there are so many missing votes that it triggers an unbalanced account for votes."

"Meaning?" Booker asked, still seeking clarity.

"Meaning if the unaccounted votes can decide a winner, which in this case is possible. Then the votes *must* be tallied."

"Damn," Booker said, lowly. "So why go through with all of this then?"

"Anything is possible, man. We always see things through and as I said earlier, we-are-winners. We're using this exposure to be front runners for 2028."

"Four years?" Booker asked aloud, shaking his head.

"To be honest with you Book, President Obama won the 2008 election in 2004 at the DNC. That's the speech that put him on the radar."

"True," Booker confessed.

"Just like the POTUS 2024 race puts you on the radar in 2028," Jasmine said. Her tone visibly moved him like a push.

"Four years is a long time." Booker sounded defeated.

"Not as long as you think," Isaac added. Think of this as rookie minicamp. Training camp is the 2028 presidential race, and the season starts Inauguration Day 2029."

"Wow." Was all Booker could say.

"You thought you'd beat Madam Vice President and our most polarizing president to date in fourteen days?" Isaac asked.

"You-damn-right." Booker laughed confidently after saying those three words individually. "Y'all are winners. You had me sold."

"We certainly are, Booker. Just so that we're clear. We presented you with two possible scenarios when we first spoke. This is not a loss. This is an exhibition. 2028 we're the main event. If we don't win then, *that's* a loss. Right now, we win no matter the outcome. This is just…" Isaac paused to think for a second. "Discounted publicity and any publicity is good publicity.

"You got millions worth of publicity for $25K. That's what we paid to get things jumpstarted, $25K. The rest was on the house. Their dime.

"As far as the PAC, it has a subaccount in your name. Whatever is left over, follows you to the next election. There are only three ways it dissolves to the RCTP.

"One is if you breach contract. The other is if you go on a campaign run with another party or independently. Lastly, if you sit out two full calendar years of elections from January to January. So technically, your clock hasn't even started yet."

"Wow!" Was Booker's first reply as he smiled. "Honestly, that's why I can't be mad or complain. I'd still be getting boo'd off hills without y'all. So, thank you. Real shit, I really appreciate y'all," he said. His voice was fluctuating in volume as he held back his emotions. Sitting still, he kept shaking his head up and down.

"No, thank you, Booker." Isaac spoke calmly but was full of passion. "Thank *you*!" He repeated. "I was all but set to retire until I saw you in front of the Joe Louis Monument. That made me want to keep pushing another eight years for your *real* campaign run in 2028 and your reelection in 2032. You have what it takes to lead this country like no other president in history."

Booker tilted his head as Isaac finished. "Balls…" Claudine, Julene, Jasmine, and Lenice all shook their heads as if asked a question.

Their unison on the subject made Booker laugh at reality. "Yeah." He agreed. "I won't deny it."

Everyone laughed, patting Booker on the back and shoulders as they returned to their seats. Booker sat silently, looking out the window for the last half hour of the flight.

As the plane descended, Booker was still quiet. Taking it all in for possibly the last time. Landing to the runway with grace, the jet slowed to a halt.

Jasmine gave clear cut instructions before leaving the plane so to stay on schedule. "Welcome home, Booker," she said to start her speech. "We have to head straight to the Bernhard Center on Western Michigan's campus to vote and we only have forty minutes to get there. Norman has already started loading our bags. We'll be leaving as soon as we touch ground."

"Touch ground, touchdown." Booker compared the two with his hands. "I see what you did there." He joked.

Norman drove across town five miles above the limit and arrived in fifteen minutes. "Alright," Jasmine said, galvanizing the troops. "7:35. Manny, you're going in first this time," she instructed. "Take a picture of us all posing for the money shot. Then I want you to record us walking in. Booker, you're front and center," she said as Booker took his spot.

"Monica." Jasmine prepared her next. "You and I will be behind Booker with you to the right of him and me on the left. Isaac to the outside of me with Julene doing the same behind Monica. Claudine and Lenice will be in the window spaces behind Booker. With Norman behind Julene to the outside. The same way we are up front. Spread out so that everyone can be seen."

Taking their places, Manny went ahead to capture the moment as they walked through the lobby. "That's B-O-O-K-E-R G-A-R-V-E-Y and three capital letter I's. Write me in y'all," he said.

Walking into a round of applause, he started the university's fight song. "Fight on, fight on for Western…" He shouted, handing over his ID to be checked in as they all sang.

"Onward for the brown and gold!" They continued.

Manny followed Booker and took footage from various angles until it ended with them touching their toe, yelling, "Go Broncos!"

Trailing him to the voter's box, Manny recorded Booker voting for himself in 4K. Next, Booker inserted the large folder into the verification machine as he awaited its approval. After receiving the OK, he picked out a sticker and stuck it to the back of his license.

No one followed his lead, prompting Booker to ask, "How y'all gon vote?"

"We already did, Dear. Absentee." Jasmine informed him.

"Same." Manny nodded.

Walking out of the voting area to another applause, Booker noticed some of his fraternity brothers. "Blu, Blu, Blu, BLU-PHI!" He shouted in a call and response pattern.

"U, U, U, U-KNO!" They echoed, coming over to see who it was.

Booker greeted members with their fraternal handshake until Manny yelled in a loud, steady, tone, "Phi Beta Sigma got…"

"SOUUUL!" They all said, gradually growing in volume until they repeated it as one and started stepping.

Handing the camera to Jasmine, Manny joined his fraternity brothers as they yelled, "P-H-I! B-E-T-A! SI-G-MA! Phi Beta Sigma!" In unison.

"BLUUU PHIII!" Booker called out.

"UUU KNOOOOO!" They all answered, strongly.

Jasmine stood in awe, "They never found out." Booker shrugged, chuckling.

"Give it more than two weeks next time." She laughed, slapping his arm. "No, that was good because you're in shape. You didn't look old and slow out there."

"Thanks." He laughed, catching his breath.

"You either, Manny. I didn't know you were a Sigma."

"U KNO!" He said with emphasis, holding up the fraternity's hand sign. "What can I say?" He asked with his palms faced up to the sides of him like J.J. Evans.

"See how that works, Booker? I would've never guessed." She laughed.

Students in the Bernhard Center asked for pictures and autographs the entire walk to the parking lot. Norman got everyone settled in and pulled off for their celebration dinner in Downtown Kalamazoo. It was at a newly opened event hall on East Michigan Avenue.

The large glass window on the front of the building led to many pedestrians peeking in throughout the day. The flashing lights inside had been going on since the polls closed at eight o'clock with a fog machine refreshing the room every half hour.

With a parking spot reserved at the entrance for the Sprinter. Norman opened the door for everyone as they reached the building. Booker looked around, nodding his head in approval. There were pictures of him on a long dinner table, videos of his speeches and early antics were projected on the wall.

Laughing on sight, he noticed a six-foot cardboard cutout of him shouting into his megaphone. He was standing atop a three-foot paper mâché crafted hill with the city of Grand Rapids behind him. "This is hilarious. I gotta take this with me." He laughed again.

Handing their jackets to the coat check attendant, Booker was down to his suspenders, shirt, and tie from his speech in Oakland. Taking a seat at the table, menus were passed around while memories began pouring out.

Election projections and results were being displayed. "It's looking bad." Booker stood up and walked over to the TV screen by the refreshments to get a better look at the latest updates.

"What needs to happen to trigger this unique scenario?" Booker asked Isaac from across the room.

Isaac walked over to tell Booker what was going on. "There are multiple ways to activate the situation, mathematically. It really depends on how things turnout. There are five hundred thirty-eight total electoral college votes. Two seventy changes everything. That triggers the need to count the votes.

"Another being that there must be a tie with you holding the needed Electoral College votes to break the tie. Hopefully the House does the right thing *if* you tie.

"At one point, third parties represented as high as 27% of the votes. The number slowly dipped as more votes came in."

"Ay, if we own fifteen to twenty something percent of that, I'll hold onto my faith!" Booker shouted as he warmed up the dance floor like James Brown.

"Get down, James." Julene smiled. Walking up to Booker, dancing in front of him, "Make room for me," she said.

Booker laughed as he made way for her. "Yes ma'am." He grabbed her hand to twirl her.

"Booker, I hope you come back for another round with us in 2028. The race is wide open. Honestly speaking, unless Madam Vice President runs again…" She paused to look him in the eye.

"It's your race to lose. Just show face from time to time over the next two years and we'll pick things back up in 2027 to do it properly. This was no good," she said.

Shaking her head, it looked as though she tasted something sour. "It was a rush job."

"Really? I couldn't tell."

"Booker, please." Julene rolled her eyes, windmill like. "Venues, stadiums, arenas, and outdoor speaking engagements. That's what we do. Not portable tents."

"Word?" Booker asked out of shock. I thought that was our thing." He admitted.

"Nooo, Booker. We only did that because we had to. We only had two weeks to put this whole thing together, fourteen days. Every venue we tried was booked."

"Where there's a will, there's a way!" Booker shouted, holding hands with Julene as they danced at a distance, bouncing to the beat. "I would've thought that was the plan if you didn't tell me."

"Oh no, Booker. We do everything spectacular. In 2024, we dropped the ball."

"Naw, I dropped the ball. I feel like if I filled out my paperwork, things would be different."

"Maybe. But Booker, stop," Her tone shifted to one of encouragement. "We had fourteen days to put this whole thing together. Feel proud of what you've accomplished so soon."

"Yes ma'am."

"Alright, go ahead and dip me so I can go about my business." She requested.

Booker hugged and dipped her backwards as everyone clapped. They all joined them, dancing to the next song in hustle formation.

Booker sat out with mediocre dancing skills and commentated what was going on instead. "I see you Jasmine, Lenice!" He said, studying their footwork. Look at Isaac." He pointed to Manny.

Isaac was having his way with the dance floor. "Aight, Isaac!" Manny shouted, cheering him on while Isaac pointed at Manny's camera lens.

Walking over to the middle of the table. It was the only spot with resting feet, Booker grabbed Claudine and Monica's hands, walking with them to the dance floor.

"Uhn uhn, Booker. No." Claudine playfully refused, standing to her feet.

"C'mon y'all! We gotta end the night with a bang." Monica stood up, squeezing Booker's hand. She rubbed the bottom half of his palm with her thumb as they approached the dance floor.

Releasing their hands, Monica's grip felt like she didn't want to let go. Booker smiled as the music changed. "Down, down, do your dance." The music played as everyone got excited, joining in. Booker walked around boosting everyone's ego as the hype man.

"Yeaaah!" Booker looked into the camera, pointing behind him to the dance floor doing his own dance.

Another song switch brought out his dancing shoes. "To the right… take it back now, y'all," the speakers went as Booker jumped in.

"I know this one." He chuckled as he danced his way in between Claudine and Monica

"I would hope so." Monica laughed.

"It's simple enough." Claudine added, laughing.

Time passed, genres changed, and laughter served as the night's soundtrack. "If this world were mine," was being mixed into play next while Monica got ready for it. Hearing it was a newly sampled version, she lost her excitement. "I thought this was Luther." Her shoulders hunched, matching her facial expression.

"It is." Booker laughed over the music, drawing attention to the two of them. "Tryna play my dawg, Kendrick."

"No, I like Kendrick." She insisted. "But I *love* Luther. I grew up on Luther." She explained with her hands directing her speech.

"You just wanted to slow dance, huh?"

"Maybe." Monica giggled.

"Claudine's hip," he said, admiring her dancing feet.

"Boy please." Claudine dismissed Booker's praise, continuing to two-step to the beat with an occasional spin, twist, wave, or slide. Saying, "I'm only up here because I was summoned."

She pat Booker's arm, "And I've fulfilled my obligations. I need some water." Claudine walked towards the refreshments.

With Booker and Monica side by side, he asked for her hand. "You still wanna slow dance?" He asked.

"Maybe." Monica's blushed cheeks matched her pink lipstick as she took hold to Booker's hands.

The two didn't dance too close or too long at all. The song changed as soon as they engaged in motion. "Damn!" Booker missed the moment.

"Sounds like you're the one who wanted to slow dance." She noticed.

"You damn right." He admitted.

"You're so extra." Monica laughed at Booker. He was still acting out his words.

"I'll be that." He shrugged, laughing.

"Well, I don't know many people who talk on dance floors. So, what are we doing here?"

Booker and Monica danced for a couple songs. Nothing sensual, mostly party anthems. They started yelling out, "Ballin!" Shooting jump shots at the basket. Then, took a seat to catch their breath and converse.

"So... why politics, Booker Garvey III? You're a teacher and an author. Why not stick to that?"

"Honestly, I just did it to sell books."

Monica interrupted him with laughter. "You did?"

"In the *beginning*!" He emphasized. "I really did want to be president in 5th grade, but my Pops told me," Booker added bass to his voice. "You can do anything except be president."

"He really told you that?" She continued laughing.

"Yeah." He chuckled. "I believed it until Obama won. It was true until Obama won."

"Well, I think you can do anything you put your mind to, Booker Garvey III."

"My type of lady." He smiled at her.

Monica smiled back, pretty political. "Sooo, we did all of this to help you sell books?" Monica asked. She was looking for a more in-depth answer.

"Those speeches had to have come from somewhere." She insisted.

"I honestly thought I'd cook Trump and Biden. Then Kamala entered the race and stole my entire voting base. But initially, I ran because I felt I could lead the country better than either of them."

"Now we're getting there. Lead the country where? To do what?"

"Americans aren't serious about shit anymore. Muh fuckas just wanna do freaky shit, get likes, views, and laugh all damn day."

"Yeah." She agreed, giggling.

"I just want to remind the boys and men how to be a man's man again. Unapologetically.

"Fuck a man's man. I want to remind them how to be a man like what we saw growing up in the '90's. It's a lot of big ass boys out here and you know I ain't lying."

"Amen!" Monica agreed.

"See, I knew it wasn't just me. I feel like if the stage is big enough, I can change the world just by reminding them how things used to be. I mean, I love change if it's evolution. But we're going backwards in some ways." Booker shook his head.

"We live in a world now where a muh fucka's opinion will outweigh facts. I'm not for that goofy shit."

Monica was fully engaged while Booker continued. "Nobody else seems to give a fuck. So, I'm fighting for my unborns. Because a couple years ago, I watched a muh fucka turn into a got damn mermaid or some shit."

Monica laughed. "I cannot."

"Real shit though." Booker chuckled, saying, "Then swam laps around two Olympians. Two, silver medalists and nobody did a mutha fucking thing!" Booker was passionate.

"So *that's* why you ran for president if anyone asks. To restore order. *Not* to sell books. That comes with it. *Balance the Scale* was perfect for you."

Booker and Monica talked all night until Isaac directed everyone's attention to the news as it displayed on the wall. With the US map decorated red and blue, Booker's fate was all but sealed. "Well, everyone. As we get closer to midnight, this show will continue shortly at the Radisson. It is time to vacate the premises. You don't have to go home, but you have to get out of here!" Isaac shouted into the microphone.

With such a small group, they were able to pack up and leave rather quickly. Less than a mile away from their next stop, they arrived in five minutes time. Norman handled bags and luggage while Monica took care of lodging per usual.

The elevator ride to the penthouse suite was a quiet one until Booker noticed, "Y'all look sad as shit," he said as the doors opened.

"People scream on rollercoasters. But when the ride is over... so are the screams," Isaac replied.

"Damn, Isaac," Booker said, admiring the line he just heard. "I thought I was deep."

"Two things can be true."

Booker nodded quietly having received the memo. "It's easy to see I'm the rookie, huh?" Booker questioned the room as everyone exited the elevator in favor of the living room in front of the TV.

"Why's that?" Jasmine asked.

"Because I'm still on a high and y'all act like it's the end of democracy."

"Well," Monica replied. "Who's to say it's not?"

Everyone shook their heads knowing what they were up against. "Don't worry about that shit. He was just trying to get elected... I think," Booker said.

Unfolding a chocolate peppermint from dinner that he pocketed. He chewed it quickly saying, "Deezam! I feel like I let the team down."

"Don't," Monica added quickly.

"Absolutely not." Julene insisted. "The *only* thing you've done, is make the team proud."

"She's right. That's why it's so gloomy, Dear. Like you said in Oakland, this was a fun ride." Jasmine plopped down to the couch, frowning.

"Sho ya right," Isaac agreed.

"I'm trying to tell him." Jasmine picked up where she left off. "We don't usually have this much fun on the campaign trail. Not *woo hoo!* Fun, of course." She demonstrated her words, raising her hands.

"An optimistic fun. We knew there was a glimmer of hope to pull it off and any port in the storm will do.

"Vice President Harris just got started in July." She explained and continued. "Her early success came for many reasons. Mainly being that she's the vice president. Endorsements from current and former presidents doesn't hurt either. Not to mention the Obamas helping her out on the campaign trail.

"That's not the point. The point is, Booker, you made a name for yourself in your first two weeks on the job."

"I keep telling people this won't hit me until later, but I think later might be happening right now." Booker sat in silence for a moment, shaking his head.

The room remained silent as their attention slowly shifted towards the TV screen. Twenty minutes went by with the only voices spoken coming from the television.

The next commercial break was a segue for Booker's exit. Looking into the refrigerator, he opened a bottled water and took a trip to his room.

Booker looked through his duffle bag, removing a box of cards and his portable speaker. Opening the Apple Music app on his phone, he made his way back to the living room.

Grabbing the TV remote from the couch, Booker muted the volume as everyone looked his way. "This ain't no funeral. Democracy isn't dead and it ain't dying either. Look," he said, holding two things in front of him. "We have music and Uno cards. We don't have to watch this being all sad n'shit."

Booker shuffled the cards as a bass drum played to a steady beat. Followed by steady taps of the Hi-Hats and a well-timed, "If this world were mine." He sang, headed towards Monica on the couch.

Booker put the speaker in the center of the coffee table ahead of them. Squeezing between Monica and Claudine, "Watch my fanny. Watch my fanny." He made his way to a seat, putting his arms around both of them.

Everyone sang song after song to old school hits of the 60s, 70s, 80s, and 1990s while the cards were played.

"Are we staying up to see who wins? Because I'm getting sleepy." Lenice got up from her seat.

"What time are we leaving? I'm trying to see if I'm headed to bed or not myself." Claudine asked, seeking clarity.

"Good question." Lenice responded.

"Y'all leaving?" Booker asked inside a ball of confusion.

"Uh, yeah," Jasmine replied. "That's another reason everyone is so sad. The ride is over, Booker. Nobody lives here but you."

Monica dropped her head, quickly catching it to rest her chin on the palm of her hand. "You *did* say, *Welcome home Booker*. You never said *we're home*." Booker sighed in his seat.

"Damn, I guess the ride is over. What time y'all leaving? That is a good question, huh?" Booker looked shocked. "Who's leaving first and where to?" He asked.

Holding the cards preparing to shuffle and deal, Booker waited to listen to everyone's response. "They all live in D.C." Monica answered first. "I live in Prince George's County, in Maryland."

"I was about to move to PG County." Booker reminisced on times that could've been.

"Really?"

"I had an offer to teach there my first year."

Monica stared at Booker unbeknownst to herself until she found herself turning away as he looked towards her. "Depends on where you would've been. We could've crossed paths or never known each other existed. I live in Bowie."

"How many cities are in PG County?" He asked.

"Twenty-seven. It's almost a million of us there."

"How y'all rep a whole county? Y'all make it sounds like it's a few cities." Booker laughed at his ignorance. "That's like me rep'n Wayne County. I'm from HP!" He said, making the two letters using his fingers.

"Don't hate, don't hate." Monica said with her hands.

"Y'all all on the same flight?" Booker asked.

"Yep. The jet will be on the runway when we get there. Twelve o'clock." Monica started biting the dead skin from her bottom lip.

"Twelve o'clock? Damn." Booker rubbed his forehead feeling his emotions tumble in front of him.

"I'm getting sleepy," Claudine said, bumping Jasmine with her elbow.

Jasmine stretched her arms and legs from a seated position, then said, "Me too."

"Hey Claudine, did I show you the pictures from dinner tonight?" Manny asked, walking off.

"I've been sleepy." Isaac, said. Then he left with Lenice and everyone else except Julene, who sat quietly.

"I know you all are grown, and I don't mean any harm in what I'm getting ready to say." Julene moved closer to Booker and Monica, closing the gap between them."

"But I think you two would look fabulous together. See you in the morning." Julene hugged them both goodnight and went on her way.

"I definitely thought she was about to cut into us." Booker put his arm around Monica while she readjusted herself to lay on his ribcage.

"I've been working with the RCTP since undergrad. I was an intern during the '06 elections, and I've been on staff ever since. I volunteered before that. I've worked part time and I've been working full time for almost fifteen years now."

"Remember the girl who introduced Michelle Obama?" She asked.

"Yeah."

"I was her at Bowie instead of Western Michigan and it wasn't the Democrats behind me. It was the Realist Critical Thinking Party. I just *knew* a lecture was coming. She watched me grow up. I've seen them come a *long* way and I mean a *long* way." Monica smiled, shaking her head.

"Word? That's a first impression for yo ass. I figured it was always like this."

"Oh no. I started two years before Isaac and Jasmine got here. They really turned things around and brought a lot of experience to the RCTP. Before that, we were kinda like you were."

"What's that mean?" Booker asked, raising his eyebrow.

"Struggling." Monica laughed under Booker's arms as she continued. "When you flipped that megaphone." Monica covered her mouth, laughing as she looked back at Booker. "Booker, I laughed harder than I am right now. I'm surprised you didn't hear me."

"I heard all y'all," Booker looked at Monica out the side of his eye and wrapped his other arm around her.

"Where were you?" He asked kissing her cheek, a few times. Then the back of her ear.

"Booker," she said. Pausing, her body shook for a second. Booker relaxed and asked her to continue. "My bad, Baby. You were dissing me getting boo'd and letting me know where y'all were."

"Right, that part," she said, taking a deep breath. "We were parked right next to the hill on the other side. We could hear and see everything. That's how we found you."

"How?" Booker asked, waiting on the answer to his million-dollar question.

"It's funny now that I think about it. When you were up there yelling, *LO-TT 48-203*... I still remember it, so I guess it worked."

"Seeee!" Booker kissed her cheek again.

"I guess so." She lifted her cheek to be kissed again.

Booker obliged. "Isaac looked at LOTT's website and like their work. Then he saw your shows and acting skills and said you looked familiar and that he read a few of your books. That's when he put two and two together with the blue megaphone. He said you had enough of what it took to *make some noise*. That's all Isaac wanted to do. *Make some noise*. You did that. You go boy!" Monica turned towards him, "Can I ask you something?"

What's up?" He stared into her eyes.

"What's going to happen when I get back to Maryland?"

"We're going to keep in touch."

"For how long?"

"What you mean?"

"You don't really like me. You *think* you like me. But you don't even really know me," she said, simply put.

"I don't. But our chemistry makes it feel like I do."

"It does. I like you, Booker." Monica turned back the way she was. "But as far apart as we are, I already know it won't last. You'll call a lot at first. Then every once in a while. After that I'll only hear from you on birthdays and holidays then not at all.

"Two, three, four years will pass, and we'll be right back in each other's face all over again. But..."

"Aw shit."

"Yea." She squinted her eye closest to him. "I'm like Kamala. I am not going back so make sure this is what you want to do, Booker." She turned around to point in his face.

Booker was blown away by the accuracy of her statement. Finding the right words to say afterwards was a tough task. Booker was aghast.

"I know whatever I feel for you makes me feel like a high schooler again. I like yo ass too. What the fuck you want me to say, Monicala?"

She laughed as he continued. "I like you too." Booker squeezed Monica in his arms as she giggled. "It's hard to say because I *don't* believe in long distance relationships."

"Seeee!" Monica imitated Booker in the tone he used.

"But it's also hard to say because I do like yo ass and wanted you the first time I saw you. Then when you said *Mrs.* Jarreau like that all those times. I went about my business and never thought about it again. You made it very clear that you wanted no parts."

"No, I just know you're a flirt."

"How you know that!?" Booker refused to believe what he was hearing.

"I was in Grand Rapids, Booker. I saw it." Monica laughed at Booker's *Flirt Mode* being in autopilot. "We all saw it."

"Damn, seriously?"

"Seriously. Anyone close to you in line went home and told whoever they saw about the man who got booed off the hill. That man is Booker Garvey III!" Monica clapped, whistled, and cheered.

"I'll take it." Booker laughed and attempted to answer the question again. "I think because I like you, I'd find time to make time."

"On the phone or a flight?"

"Both."

Booker kissed Monica's cheek again and again, then behind her ear and on her neck. Then he nibbled her ear.

"Booker, you better stop." Monica turned around again and kissed his lips.

Sitting upright, their lips were tied. "Don't... start something... you can...'t... finishhh," she said when she could.

"I can't start something without finishing." He confessed.

"Oooh." Monica smiled, breathing heavily in Booker's ear. "You so badd." She whispered.

"Damn yea," he said, looking at her in his arms. "I'll be that."

"Damn yeah?"

"I make up my own catch phrases and cuss word arrangements n'shit." Booker shrugged.

"Why am I not surprised." Monica laughed as she got more comfortable in his arms. "What about them?" She asked, nodding down the hallway of the penthouse suite.

"What about them?" Booker chuckled with a shrug. "Julene said we're grown, and we all know what grownups do."

Booker started kissing her again. She turned around and mounted herself on his lap, facing him. The temperature of the room rose rapidly without much change in degrees. Kissing, their tongues waved like water.

Booker stood up as Monica wrapped her legs around his waist. "Don't hurt me, Booker. Please don't hurt me. I don't have sex just because." She whispered in his ear, kissing and licking around it.

The penthouse suite was setup like the midpoint of a hotel floor. The elevator separated the penthouse in half. With four large rooms to the left and right of it.

The living room was straight ahead with the kitchen and dining room being on opposite sides. Norman, Jasmine, Julene, and Isaac were down the hall on the right side of the elevator. With Claudine, Manny, Monica, and Booker over to the left.

The living room was steaming and its occupants were migrating. Walking with Monica's legs still wrapped around his waist. He held her upper body, kissing her the entire way.

Booker took a breath to say, "Grab the door."

Monica reached behind her to turn the doorknob then closed it behind them with her foot. The rooms were hotel rooms that had been remodeled for the penthouse suite. They all had separate bathrooms, a mini fridge, and microwave.

"This is like having our own room anyway," Booker said. Easing her down to the bed, he laid her on her back.

"Huuuu," Monica exhaled in Booker's ear, holding his head. She was no longer able to speak.

"They won't hear you," he assured her. "Unless they hear you." He looked at her with a side eye.

"Oh, Bookerrr," she said as they began kissing again.

Kissing led to touching and touching turned into much more. With Monica on her back, Booker undressed her.

He unstrapped her bra as a pair of 34C breast spread across her chest. Booker pulled down her underwear as she lifted her butt in the air.

Curling her like a barbell, he lifted her off the bed and into his arms, carrying her to the bathroom. Sitting her atop the counter, he stood between her legs and picked up where they left off. She removed his shirt and traced the definition of his muscles with her fingers.

Reaching the bottom of his abdomen, she tugged on his belt buckle and loosened it. Pulling down his pants and boxer briefs, she appeared to be taken back. He smirked and grabbed her hands, helping her down from the counter.

Booker picked up his pants. He reached into his pocket, removing three golden squares. He tore off one and tossed the other two on the counter.

Monica gently grabbed hold to him as he followed her to the shower. Testing the waters, she twisted the handle, adjusting the temperature. Booker slapped Monica on the butt. She looked back and grabbed hold to him again.

Kissing underneath the water shower falling from half the ceiling; Booker tore open the gold package with his teeth and tossed the wrapper. It was a condom. In one motion, he pinched it at the top and rolled it down the tip of his penis.

Lifting Monica into the air, he lowered her onto his crotch slowly and carefully. A moan escaped her mouth, immediately. Booker squatted with Monica on his lap. She sat on him similar to a backwards chair, moving up and down. Around and around. "Do that shit." He licked his bottom lip, squeezing her cheeks.

Changing positions, he told her to, "Turn around." Monica bounced on Booker's lap as he kissed and licked her back until they climaxed simultaneously. "Gooottt!" Booker warned her.

"Dayyuumm!"

"Yea!" Monica moaned. "Oh yea!" She echoed. "I'm about to cum, I'm about to cum!" She repeated as they both released.

"Aghhh!" Booker struggled as he let loose.

"Damn, Booker," she said with shaky legs as the water trickled down her back. Holding onto the wall, she moved around trying to get her balance together.

Grabbing her by the waist, Booker sidestepped through the shower door for a couple wash rags. Squirting his towel with soap from the dispenser behind him, he lathered it and washed Monica's body.

She turned around and wrapped her arms around him. Monica needed a moment before returning the favor. After washing each other, they got out the shower with Booker hugging her from behind. Kissing her softly on the way to bed.

"My clothes are in my room." She realized she hadn't gotten settled in.

Booker laughed and gave her his glow in the dark, brain T-Shirt. "You take care of my Baby, Baby," he said. Before giving her a kiss.

"This is my favorite undershirt."

"Awww, Bookerrr." She kissed him back. "Here." Reaching in between the sheets, she held her red, laced girl short panties on her finger. "And these are mine."

"Mine too." Booker smelled them and fell back to the bed. Smiling, he clutched them against his chest.

"You are so... silly." Monica laughed.

"Where you sleeping tonight?" Booker asked.

"Where do you want me to sleep tonight?"

"Shiiit, with me."

"At some point, I'm going to have to get some clothes and I don't do Walk of Shames, Mister..." She paused, looking at Booker. "So... that means you have to get my suitcase." Monica patted him on the chest.

"Me?" He asked. "What if Julene sees me?" He asked, wondering what she'd say.

"We're grown." Monica laughed. "Remember?"

"Oh, I remember," he said. Smiling at her, he shook his head. How could I forget?" Booker asked, kissing her. "Let me use the bathroom real quick and I'll go."

"Thank youuu." She started putting on Booker's T-Shirt.

"Yes'm."

POTUS 2024: BALANCE THE SCALE

Leaving the bathroom with his belongings, Booker looked in the closet for a plastic dirty clothes bag. Instead, he made a discovery. "Who's next to me? You or Manny?"

"Me."

"We got a joint room." Booker unlocked the door. "I'm getting excited for nothing. Your side has to be open, I'm sure." Opening the door, confirmed it. "Duh," he said.

"Time to take that walk." Monica giggled.

"You fun-naaay." He chuckled. Booker opened the door and closed it slowly behind him. Missing his chance to keep things between them easily by a half minute; Booker saw Isaac headed towards the kitchen and he had to think quick.

Making his way to the same place, Booker shook Isaac's extended hand. "Booker Garvey III, you have exceeded anything I saw for you and my hopes were high." Isaac had a glass of water in his other hand.

"Thanks, Isaac." Booker pat Isaac on the back after shaking hands. "I have to thank you and the RCTP for everything. I would've finished just because I'm not a quitter without y'all."

"With y'all, shiiit. I thought I had a chance until about two or three hours ago. Thinking on it, I wish we had more time like y'all said. To do what we did in two weeks is wild."

Booker stood still, shaking his head in awe, finally living in the moment. Reaching into the refrigerator, he removed five bottles of water.

"Booker, that was nothing. It was organized but it was nothing. There was a reason we told you everything last minute. We only had fourteen days." He shrugged, watching the election projections still playing on the TV.

"We couldn't do anything until you joined the RCTP. But once you did, we were all in. All hands on deck."

Booker put one of the water bottles in his sweat shorts and held the others; two in both hands, listening to every word Isaac spoke. "We were scrambling, gambling on locations we hadn't seen. Calling people we haven't spoken to in years. Even mended a few relationships because we had no choice. We had fourteen days." Isaac spoke to Booker with passion whenever they talked.

"Fourteen days," Booker repeated.

"But the only reason any of it happened was because of you, Book. I need you to understand that. We were out of the race. Not just this one but most. We're very selective. But your fire ignited ours again.

"We're all Lobbyist for the RCTP at this stage of our careers. But you brought the crew back together for our final act. A run at the White House.

"Those one hundred thirty-four victories we spoke to you about, was for probably any position you can think of. You will find someone we've managed in just about every position in politics. Every position but president because we're winners, Book.

"If we ever made a push for the White House, we said they'd have to be a Realist at heart. To the core of their being and that we'd know them when we saw him or her. Booker that was forty years ago.

"We knew it was you when we saw you. The jury is still out. But as far as POTUS 2028, you've got our full support. We don't need an answer until the end of 2025 regarding 2028 but we'll be lobbying as soon as we get back to D.C.

"By the time you get back in the game, you'll see what we mean when we called this a rush job. You made it look better than it really was."

"Damn, Isaac. If I had tears, I'd probably be crying right now. I won't be thinking about politics until I drop the book on July 5th, but I'll definitely be in touch before the end of next year.

"This was the most fun I've had in a long time. Shiiit it was *woo hoo* fun for me. This shit was a movie. I had to write a book about it. It's too easy not to."

"I don't know how entertaining it'll be." Isaac chuckled. "We've just been working and you've only had one scandal."

"Jamaica? Yeah, they caught me slipping." Booker laughed.

"Crazy thing is, I don't even like using the O-word." Booker shook his head.

"If the shoe fits. Old is a mentality and so the body follows the mind."

"That's a fact." He agreed. "I hope you know; I'm taking a lot of your cool ass sayings. Especially the one about rollercoasters."

"Use them well." Isaac chuckled.

"Yessir." Booker saluted. "Speaking of sayings, you can tell by the caption whose side they're on in that Jamaica YouTube Short video. We were *clearly* in HP or the Ren Cen when it got posted."

"True. When your competition or their supporters try to take shots at you, it means you're their competition too." Isaac nodded his head, taking another sip of water.

"Well, Booker. Job well done. You did the best you could with the hand you were dealt. Again, this was not a loss. This was an exhibition. But next time is for real… and it's ours to lose. Good night, young man. See you in the morning." Isaac shook hands as he departed and placed his glass in the sink.

Booker stalled long enough getting a paper towel for Isaac to get a head start down the hallway. By the time Booker turned the handle to Monica's door, Isaac was already in his room.

Opening the joint room door, Booker saw Monica had fallen asleep atop the covers. Slowly, she awoke to the noise he made coming in, "I thought you went home," she said.

Booker put the five water bottles in the mini fridge then made his way to bed. Monica sat up to get under the covers and Booker was right behind her. "Shit naw."

He kissed her neck over her shoulder. "You know damn well I didn't go home with you lying here half naked in my old shirt."

"Yup, yo *old* shirt." She snickered.

"You look better in it anyway. Isaac got to talking that real shit," Booker said. Then he kissed Monica's cheek. "I think I heard him laugh for the first time, too. It was like a chuckle."

"He is human, Booker." Monica snickered at Booker.

"I was supposed to holla at him about some other shit, but we ran out of time."

"2028?" Monica grinned.

"2028." He chuckled.

"Where was he, watching TV?"

Readjusting himself, Booker got in a more comfortable resting position. "I saw him going to the kitchen. So, I winged it like I was getting water."

"You got it done." Monica giggled again, turning around for a better resting spot after his movements. "Thank you." She kissed his lips and that got things started again with Booker on top. Monica moaned in Booker's ear, bit the knuckles on his fingers, and the pillow. All not to self-implode.

Rolling over, connected at the midsection, Monica was in sync with Booker's body as she straddled him. Booker grunted while the two were in motion. He groaned as she moaned. Shaking as she laid down, Booker completed their moment in unison.

Cuddling, they slept the night away. Waking up lying back-to-back, Monica's head was rested in the pit between Booker's arm and shoulder. Moving to her side of the bed, Booker rolled over and Monica laid on his chest. "Good morning," she said.

"Great morning," he replied doing a crunch to kiss her temple.

"Mmm hmm." She giggled. "Great morning to you too." She kissed his chest.

Lying still, they adjusted to the new day. After a while, Monica said, "Let me get ready for breakfast. I can smell it now."

"Let me know when you're ready."

"K," she said. Sliding her feet into her slippers, Monica put on Booker's T-shirt and began leaving his room for hers. "I'm just going to brush my teeth, put on a bra, and some pajama pants. I'll be ready in ten minutes."

"Let me see the girls one more time. It might be a while before I get to see them again." Booker sighed until she flashed him, and he was all smiles again.

A few minutes later, Monica came to the doorway to say, "K. I'm ready. Come pick me up."

Booker walked over to Monica. Hugged her then held her thighs in his hands like dumbbells. Lifting her into the air, she wrapped her legs around his waist. "Not like this." She laughed. "Out there."

"Ohhh, I got you." They kissed once more as he eased her to the ground.

Booker walked out of his room and knocked on Monica's door. Everyone was walking around and could see them coming down the hall. "Good morning," Jasmine said with everyone else.

"Good morning," Booker and Monica replied.

"Awww. She slept in his shirt. Aren't they cute?" Julene said. Her smile was radiant. It was obvious she admired them.

"They actually are." Claudine admitted.

"Aren't they?" Jasmine thought, "I didn't see it at first, but I can definitely see it now," she said. Jasmine covered her mouth as she finished chewing, pointing her egg filled fork at them.

"I'm surprised it took this long." Isaac added his two cents last.

Booker grinned boyishly and handed Monica a plate. "Now correct me if I'm wrong but, I don't remember you sleeping in a shirt last night," Booker recalled. He whispered it lowly as Monica got a spoonful of cheese eggs.

"No." She giggled. "I didn't."

Next was the turkey sausage and grits. "Aw shit…" Booker paused to see what Monica was going to do.

"What?" She asked, scooping a portion on her plate.

"I'm trying to see what you do with your grits."

"Butter and sugar," she said. Monica reached for the teaspoon sitting next to the grits and sprinkled sugar atop her plate.

"Awww dayyuuuum." Booker's body threw a tantrum. "You were almost perfect." He pinched his two fingers. "You're right about the butter," he said.

After putting a couple serving spoons on his plate, "Butter, salt, cheese, Baby. Butter, salt, and cheese." He countered.

"Then why is the cheese down there and the salt is on the table? But the sugar… is next to the grits?"

"Good question." Booker was stumped. "Must be an East Coast thing?" He questioned, shrugging his shoulders.

"Maybe." Monica giggled as they got mimosas before having a seat.

Taking the last two spots at the table, Booker sat by Manny. Putting Monica next to Julene who was at the head of the table, opposite of Isaac. "What's good, brodie?" Booker and Manny pounded fists.

Before Booker started eating, he looked to his right, asking Monica, "Can I try those grits?"

"Even without cheese?" She asked, sliding her plate towards his.

Holding his right elbow down to the table, Booker used his left hand to grab the saltshaker. He shook it a few times in his palm then held his hand up in the air. Booker sprinkled salt on his grits from a distance.

"OK," Monica said. Watching it all, laughing.

"Here, I'll trade you."

"Umm." She was a bit apprehensive.

"I'll start you off light," he said.

The grits were thick, and its temperature was hot enough to melt the cheese beneath it. Breaking up food with his fork, the cheddar cheese was stringy enough to follow his fork to her plate.

After a bite, she was pleasantly surprised. "They aren't terrible." She admitted.

"OK! That's a start," he said. Looking at his plate, he took a sip of water. "Gotta clear my taste buds," he said. Having tried the sample, he cleared his fork. "And this, tastes like dessert!" Booker was clearly confused. His eyebrows were moving and his head tilted.

"I can see why you'd say that." Monica giggled, eating from her plate.

"How'd you sleep, Sugar?" Julene asked Monica.

"Like a baby, Mrs. J." Monica laughed politely.

Bumping Booker's knee, he quickly looked Manny's way to find something to laugh at. "You?" Monica asked.

"The same. The beds were so soft." Julene recalled.

"Yesss ma'am they werrre," she said, exaggerating her speech. "I laid there for at least twenty minutes before getting out of bed this morning."

"Thirty for me." Julene smiled.

"This is it y'all," Jasmine said.

From the middle of the table, she commanded the room's attention. "It's..." Looking at her wrist, she continued. "8:09. We are out of here at 10:30 sharp or you will get left in Kalamazoo with Booker."

Looking down the table to the right, "Monica, please don't get any ideas," Jasmine said.

Laughter circulated around the table. "Dang it!" She wittily replied.

As Booker shouted, "Damn!" At the same time.

"How y'all do that already?" Manny laughed with the table.

"They even shrugged together." Isaac pointed out. Looking at the two of them separately then together, he smiled.

"This is why they haven't said anything and still haven't, really," Lenice said. Her tone was filled with impatience. "Y'all act like we're in high school."

The table found their way back to the topic soon after. "I guess you told *me*!" Jasmine folded her right hand closed towards Lenice, leaning away in rhythm. "10:30 sharp, y'all." She pointed around the table with her fork. It had a piece of turkey sausage stuck to it. Then she ate it after receiving confirmation.

Once breakfast was over, everyone went back to their rooms to pack and get ready to go their separate ways. With just under thirty minutes left, they all met up in the living room. Some of them had already been there. "We didn't even talk about Forty-Five, Forty-Seven," Booker said.

Sitting on the couch with his arm around Monica, he grabbed the remote from the cushion next to him. Then he muted the TV to give Lenice the floor.

"Now we have," Lenice said. With her legs crossed, her bouncing foot was a clear indicator that she was ready to move on.

Booker laughed nodding his head to acknowledge her point. "There it is."

"I'll show you what we should be talking about." Lenice tapped a few buttons on her phone's screen. Then she started to AirPlay a LOTT48203 YouTube playlist, featuring Booker Garvey III.

"POTUS 2024! That's what I'm talking about!" Booker was excited, clapping his hands. All Monica could do was laugh, clap and stare.

Soon enough, everyone started laughing and cheering when Booker rounded the corner in front of the Joe Louis Monument. Wearing a Honolulu blue Starter jacket. A gray number five jersey and a blue megaphone. Saying calmly yet seriously, "We need to balance the scale, y'all. For real…"

"Look at Book!" Manny shouted, clapping at the screen.

"He was so rough around the edges." Claudine smiled at his growth and progression.

"Now look at him." Monica pinched his smiling cheeks.

The playlist moved on to the next video. Manny yelled at the TV singing, "Suited and booted!" They all laughed.

I went from East Michigan to West Michigan then back east where I got a Master's degree from Eastern Michigan University in Education Administration with a 3.7gpa while teaching full time.

I'm also a writer. The greatest writer of my generation, greatest writer of my era, greatest writer of the 21st century.

Booker looked left, winking, and licking his lips on screen at a woman in the crowd. "You are something else." Monica shook her head at Booker, smirking.

"What?" He replied.

"A lion has to eat!" Isaac made a dad clap while Julene and Jasmine shook their heads.

"Do not encourage this behavior." Jasmine joked.

Next on the playlist was a powerful speech Booker had given in hopes to increase teacher pay. He also aimed to decrease the hours of the full-time school and workday.

Some teachers come to school starving and have to put on a good face in front of twenty-five students and some of which may also be starving. That's wrong. That's not right. What it's really doing is taking advantage of the loving nature of a teacher's soul.

Booker's voice played on the TV screen. He appeared presidential in his presentation. "Look how serious he is!" Lenice smiled. Saying, "I love it."

"Mmm, Mmm, Mmm..." Monica complimented, "What a man."

Booker smiled, kissing her cheek while she was under his arm.

"Awww." Jasmine started fanning her eyes. "I just can't. I've never seen Monica like this before."

Next up was Booker's public service announcement.

That might scare you away but not me. I'm a teacher and teachers don't quit on our students the same way I won't quit on our citizens.

"This turned out good," Julene said, admiring their work.

"One of the best," Isaac added.

"One take Jake!" Manny shouted.

"One take Jake!" Booker replied, shaking hands. "You bodied that."

"My dawg. Stay ready, you ain't gotta get ready." Manny said. He started shadowboxing immediately after shaking hands.

The last video on the playlist drew mixed emotions. Sadness for the last speech and anticipation for the same reason.

Good evening... My fellow Americans,

I would first like to start by thanking everybody who hopped on this journey with us. It's been a fun ride. And if this is the last time that I see you, it was great meeting you. So let's go ahead and get started, let's go ahead and get started. Aight, aight... let's keep it loose today.

This is the last time that we will be here this election season. You know, I might see some of you all in January and I might see some of you all in four years. We'll see. We'll find that out soon.

"Is this when he kept looking at Monica?" Claudine asked, seeing the speech again for the first time.

"Yup." Monica was blushing, dancing in her seat.

"I liked what I saw." Booker shrugged. "A wise man once said, *a lion has to eat!*"

"Ha!" Isaac laughed loud and quick with one loud *Clap!*

"You clean up nice, Booker." Julene smiled proudly.

"Doesn't he?" Monica agreed, looking at Booker.

"It's the glasses." Booker laughed. Recalling what happened, "Monica said I looked tired," he said.

"Good call. Makes you look smarter than you already are," Julene replied. "And you already look good in a suit."

"Thanks, Mrs. J."

Bloods, Crips, Vice Lords, GDs, Latin Kings, all of them. We invite you to the Homeland Defense. Bang for our country or not at all. We believe in your strength and together, we can get back to your organization's original roots... to protect the communities from foreign invasion.

POTUS 2024, B GARV... out!

Booker's on screen image saluted the camera to an in person, standing ovation for the man himself.

"Good job, Booker!" Monica stopped clapping to rub his back and shoulders.

"Welp, that ended right on time. Or should I say, Rydon Tyme." Jasmine made word play referencing a character from one of Booker's books.

"I see what you did there, Jazz." Booker used two fingers to point from his eyes to hers as she did the same in return.

"Ten minutes and we're leaving. Make sure you're ready. Norman is packing bags now then meeting us at the front door with the Sprinter."

Everyone stayed put while Norman retrieved their belongings to load the cart. Finishing up down the hall, he passed the elevator and started with Claudine's room. After that, he went next door to Manny's and loaded his bags on the cart.

Leaving for the next room, he opened Monica's door and packed her luggage as well. Noticing the joint door was open, he thought nothing of it. Until he entered Booker's room and saw an empty golden wrapper. It was on the floor by Booker's duffle bag, next to the bed.

Norman picked up the wrapper, balled it up and went to the bathroom to roll it in tissue. Only to find another empty wrapper on the floor by the shower. Layering the new wrapper over the other, he covered them both in tissue paper and shot it into the trash can. Saying, "Booker Garvey III," under his breath. Shaking his head, he smirked.

Leaving the penthouse suite, Norman took their bags to the Sprinter, packed it, and pulled around to the front of the hotel. It was around the same time that everyone made their way out.

The fifteen minutes it took to get to the airport was a party. "Before we board, we have some gifts for you, Book," Jasmine informed him.

"Really? Damn, I didn't get y'all anything. I legit thought y'all lived here. At least in Michigan."

"It's OK. Don't worry about it." Jasmine handed him a cylinder-shaped container and two boxes. "This must be water, he laughed popping the top. To his surprise, it was a bottle of champagne.

"Open it on July 5th," she said. "For your book release."

"Ayyye, thanks, y'all!" Reaching for the smaller box, he opened it to find a black hoody and a navy blue crewneck sweatshirt. They both read, *RCTP* across the chest with *Realist Critical Thinking Party* underneath each letter. *The Party (2024)* was on the left sleeve with their names going down the arm.

"This is cold," he said. "It has all of our names on it." Admiring the hoody and sweatshirt, he held them out in front of him.

"I might have to fly D.C. to drink this with y'all."
"Promise?" Monica blushed.
Booker did the same, saying, "I hope so?" They all laughed at the latest impersonation.
Opening the last gift was a bigger box. When he opened the box, it was another box and another box. Booker laughed. "Aight."
"Just open it." Monica smiled.
Ripping open the box, "Ohhh shit! Dayyuuuuum," was his first reply. Booker thanked everyone with hugs and a kiss for Monica. "My mutha fuck'n megaphone!" He shouted, taking it out of the box.
Powering it on, "DOES IT STILL WORK!?" He asked, projecting his voice into the receiver. Everyone on the Sprinter covered their ears from Booker's blunder.
Eleven thirty came around and started with Norman getting out to load the private jet with their bags. After doing so, he came back to the Sprinter to let everyone out.
"Next stop, Washington D.C.," he announced. Opening the sliding passenger door for the last time of the 2024 campaign. Norman left the keys in the ignition for the RCTP's replacement driver while he waited for them to clear the vehicle.
"Alright, it's time." Isaac said, exiting the Sprinter.
Crowding around Booker, they all said their goodbyes, one at a time. "Norm! Thanks!" They shook hands. "Woodgrain whip'n!" He moved like a stock car driver.

"Booker Garvey III," he replied. "The man, the myth, the legend. Thank you. I was itching to get back on the road but, I'm not the Campaign Manager of the bunch. I have to play my part in the waiting game."

"Teamwork makes the dream work, Norm." Booker shook his hand again.

While Booker moved on to Lenice, Manny bid farewell to Norman.

"Lenice!" Booker hugged her saying, "We know why you're here!" He smiled. "Because you're one of the realist muh fuckas I ever met!" He shouted.

"And you're a rising star, Booker. You can be the Sun one day even," she said as they hugged.

"Thank you, Lenice." He hugged her tighter. "Thank you... Stay on they ass like a Pamper, Lenice," he said. He held her forearms as they pulled away.

"You know I will," she said. Discreetly, she stopped a tear while adjusting her glasses.

Claudine was next up. "Claudine, thank you! You gave my dawg an opportunity." Booker hit Manny's arm behind him who was hugging Lenice goodbye. "And had me looking all political n'shit," he said, talking with his hands.

"You're great at your job. All y'all are!" Booker stepped back to look at them as a whole and shook his head in disbelief.

"Thank you, Booker. You're going to make Gen Z start thinking about politics. We are winners but you're our first political Millennial. You're going to start a wave of young politicians who do… something," she said, slow and low. "Watch what I tell you." Claudine hugged Booker's head. She was greatly appreciative."

"My dawg!" Booker shook the man's hand who invested time and energy into his potential with authority and a salute. "I wouldn't be here without you, Isaac."

Isaac tilted his head for more information.

"You recruited me!" He exclaimed.

"I wouldn't call it all of that. You stole the show. At least the pregame show. What'd you expect?" Isaac shrugged.

"No, really. Booker, you're a natural. That means you were born to do this. What we watched on screen before we left, was you accepting constructive criticism and *growing* from it. You discovered a lot about yourself, Booker." Isaac pat Booker on the back while shaking his hand.

"Jazz, I don't know where to start. I *know* I wouldn't be here without you. You're the heart and soul of The Party. You get shit done and to have that kind of force behind me." Booker shook his head. "I'll always owe you, Jazz."

"Booker hugged Jasmine as they rocked sideways. "Aww, Booker." Jasmine lost it, crying.

Monica had been tearing up since Booker talked to Isaac. The women consoled her while she cried. It all came out watching Jasmine cry during their goodbyes.

"I could say everything to you that you just told me, Booker Garvey III." Jasmine looked Booker in the eyes and said, "I'm looking at our country's next president." She smiled at him. "Four years, Booker Garvey III. Give us four years. You became the total package in fourteen days, Book. Two weeks!" She reminded him intensely, hugging him once more.

"Fourteen days," Isaac echoed in the background.

"Thanks, y'all. For real. It's really about to hit me now." Hugging Julene, he said, "I'm almost out of goodbyes." Booker looked at Monica over Julene's shoulder.

"Mrs. J, I really want to thank you for giving me the opportunity. I'm learning how the political game works one day at a time. For you to green light all of this before any checks were cleared, that means a lot. Y'all must really think we can do this thing." He smiled, holding her arms.

"Booker, this was not a big bill, at all. It may seem like a lot in a two-week span. But the most expensive election expense is marketing. You didn't need but a nudge to get the ball rolling.

"You're a media darling, handsome." Julene pinched through Booker's bearded cheek. "They need you more than you need them. The pleasure was ours. The pleasure *is* ours," she said. Julene hugged him tightly before letting go.

The ladies let Monica go to be with Booker while they conversed amongst themselves. "Aww, Monica's all grown up now," Claudine said. Walking towards the plane with Isaac and Norman, she was the first to address things.

"I know, right?" Jasmine joined her.

"I can't believe y'all." Lenice was right behind them with Julene, shaking her head.

"Here comes the hard part," Julene said.

Monica walked towards Booker, sobbing with her arms opened for a hug. She cried in his arms as he rubbed her back. "If we're hugging during my goodbyes, that means you're headed back to Bowie. I saved the best for last."

Booker kissed Monica passionately and affectionately. Monica's hands roamed Booker's torso before resting, holding his arms. They wrapped things up momentarily to finish their conversation.

"I mean, PG County." Booker joked as she laughed through her tears.

"I'm going to miss you." Monica giggled, blushing with running mascara and smeared lipstick. "I miss you already and I'm still here. Booker, I don't want to leave." She cried into his chest.

"I don't want you to leave either."

"Booker, that doesn't change anything." Sniffling, she looked into his eyes. "What if we never see each other again?"

"Shiiit." He dismissed while she was still saying his name. "The only way that happens is if you curve me. You got my nose open." Booker flared his nostrils. "Wide open."

"I'm really gonna miss laughing with yo silly self."

Locked at the pelvis with his fingers locked atop her backside, staring eye to eye, Booker took a deep breath. His breathing skipped as he built courage. "Monica, I've never felt this way about anybody this fast in a long time."

"You telling me." She laughed, wiping her eyes with the Kleenex Jasmine had given her.

"Something about you makes me feel like you're mine and I'm yours, already."

"Booker, what are you saying?" She asked, still wiping her eyes and nose.

"Shit, I don't know. But I think I love you, Monica." Booker was telling all.

"I wanted to say it so bad last night but didn't know how or if I should even," she said. "It's not like we've been talking for two weeks. It's been what, a day? Barely. Are we crazy?" She asked. "Because I think I love you too, Booker. I almost know it."

"I don't know what the fuck we are. But I almost know it too…" Booker paused. "Might've been love at first sight for me." He confessed.

"It was knowing it could've been the last sight for me," she said.

They began kissing on the runway again. Already behind schedule, it was time for the two to part ways. Everyone gathered by them one last time since neither had yet to let go of each other. "Text, calls, FaceTime, and flights, right?" Monica asked.

"Text, calls, FaceTime, and flights. You damn right. TCFF, t-cu-ff!" Booker said, trying to pronounce the acronym as a word.

Monica laughed as he walked her to the jet. He propped his arm open with his elbow bent to walk her up the stairs. "Booker, what are you doing?" Monica laughed, still teary eyed.

"Sending you off right!" Booker kissed Monica's hand, walked her up the stairs and straight to the snack bar. He made her a plate of fresh fruit, snagged an orange juice and a bottled water for her on the way.

Escorting Monica to her section, Booker held her hand, easing her to a seat. Fastening Monica's seatbelt, he caressed the back of her head at the neckline to kiss her goodbye.

"Text me when you land and call me when you get home," he said. Holding the back of her head in his hands like a cantaloupe, he kissed her once more on the frontal lobe.

"Um hmm." She agreed, trying her best not to cry again, smiling with her eyes closed.

Booker walked away saluting The Party saying, "2028!"

"2028!" They all replied, waving with Monica blowing kisses.

"Can't Wait!" Isaac shouted with one loud clap.

"Me either!" Monica wailed.

Booker ducked under the doorway of the jet's door and walked down the boarding stairs, smiling.

Headed towards Manny, Booker stood next to him on the runway as the private jet prepared for takeoff. Pulling off on wheels, it started a turn to bend the corner before heading towards the straightaway.

He reached into his pocket for the LOTT phone line. Recording the RCTP's departure, Booker captured the jet taking off towards the Sun.

Walking back to the Sprinter, the RCTP already had a replacement driver there to take them back to Booker's condo. The ride was a quiet one. Both of them looked out the customized tinted windows and moonroof in a daze for most of it.

As they got ready to exit the vehicle, Booker asked, "Was that shit a dream, bro?"

Reaching Booker's residence, the driver unpacked everything and gave Booker a small manila envelope. "What's this?" Booker asked. "A bill?"

The driver laughed quickly before saying, "No, sir. I'm not sure what it is. It was on top of your bag. But I promise it's not a bill."

"I was about to say." Booker laughed it off.

"You two take care."

"You too," they replied.

Manny stood on the walkway to the condominium, recording Booker's last interaction with the RCTP and the Sprinter as they watched the van drive away.

Manny stopped the video of the Sprinter driving away once it was out of sight. He sent the footage to Booker and The Party's group chat, then put his phone back in his pocket.

"That shit was a lot of things, brodie. A dream it t'was not. I had to wait to see if that was a bill before I answered." He laughed before saying, "I got enough footage for a movie, a documentary *and* a blooper reel."

"I know you do. You were all over the place. In the crowd with muh fuckas." Booker shook his head just thinking about it.

"Drop an Election Day promo video. Maybe a minute or two and a highlight reel of quotes and one liners for book promo. You can put the rest in the vault until we come back for POTUS 2028 next year." Booker and Manny bumped fists.

"Got you."

Taking the penthouse elevator, they reached the top floor. Migrating to the living room, they debriefed immediately. "What's that?" Manny asked. The only thing left in Booker's hands was the envelope.

POTUS 2024: BALANCE THE SCALE

"I don't know. The driver said it was on top of my bag."

Booker opened the envelope finding two payroll checks, a handwritten note, and the poll results with *fourteen days*, stapled to it. One of the checks read $11,000 with a $1,000 per day rate. The other showed $16,438.50 with a note paperclipped to it.

Wednesday, November 6, 2024

Booker,

I told you if you didn't win, we'd pay you the presidential rate. Presidents make $400,000 per year. That's about $1,095.90 per day, for 15 days (10/23-11/6). Although we did not lose... We didn't win. I should've watched my wording.

Stay sharp,
Isaac Van Sertima

"Not only was it not a dream... but we got paid for that shit, bro." Manny read the check repeatedly. Each time with wider eyes. "Bro, when you said ten bands. I'm not gon say I thought you were gas'n. But I fasho thought it was a mistake. I'm like maybe he meant a *couple* bands."

Booker laughed while Manny continued. "For real bro, eleven bands? They paid me eleven bands for eleven days of work?" Manny took pictures of both sides of the check and deposited into his checking account swiftly. The check deposit feature on his bank's app was able to confirm the RCTP's validity on the spot.

"That shit worked, bro. It's already included in my available balance." Manny showed Booker his phone.

"Manny, bro. Act like you've been here." Booker reminded him.

"Or anywhere we go." Manny joined in as they finished the last line together, laughing for a moment.

"I'm scared to deposit mine," Booker said. "I spend money for no reason." Booker shook his head. "I might get a G Wagon."

"They start out at one fifty." Still navigating through his banking app, Manny was already done paying bills for the rest of the year. After transferring money to his savings account, he got off the app in peace.

"Word? Damn!" Booker shouted. "I'ma have to sell some more books."

He laughed with Manny then read the attached polling results aloud, rounding most the numbers. "Trump 77.3 milli, Madam VP 75 milli, J Stein 782K, Kennedy 756K, Oliver 641K."

Included in the listings was his name, "Booker Garvey III!" He shouted. Before reading, he could only laugh. "My birthday? C'mon dawg. You can't make this shit up, one hundred eighteen thousand, seven hundred eighty-seven. 1-1-8-7-8-7." He finished reading the paper and handed it to Manny.

"I'ma keep it a bean with you, bro," Manny said. Looking at the numbers, he continued. "I ain't never known you to be a liar but if I wasn't with you and you told me what happened, I'd only be able to believe maybe half of what you told me, tops. If any of it, bro, and that's after seeing you on the news." Manny shook his head in awe.

"Mannn, I barely believe it myself and I lived the shit... on camera!"

"I know you got your book bread, but we hopped in and out of custom PJs like cars, bro. Like cars!"

"Mannn," Booker said, again. "Book bread is cool when the book first drops and random spurts after that. Two books sold enough to get a condo and a truck. The rest make enough to travel when I can but not on a PJ. I don't even fly first class."

"You might have to now, bro."

"I hope not."

"So..." Manny said. He stalled long enough to set the stage whenever he was ready. "While we're in disbelief. Monica... How? When? Where was I?"

Booker laughed before saying anything. Then was very careful with what he said next. "What you mean, bro?" He asked.

"You know what I mean. How you pull that off?"

"Honestly, bro. I don't know my damn self. I bullshit you not. It *just* started Election Day."

"Election Day? That was yesterday." Manny was confused. "You saying, y'all just started showing it yesterday?"

Booker laughed, trying to explain by saying less. "Before yesterday's speech, we realized we might never see each other again. Then I found out she wasn't married. She shot me down three times the first time I met her. Talking about, *Mrs.* Jarreau." Booker laughed recalling their introduction.

"She told me, Mrs. Monica. Ain't that a bitch?" Manny shook his head. "I knew she wasn't married though. She don't even wear her ring half the time and sometimes it be on her other hand."

"See, I didn't catch it. She shot me down so quick. I tried my best to ignore her badd ass. It was her Granny's ring. She said she wears it to keep muh fuckas from trying her so much."

"I bet. She cold, dawg. You got lucky."

"Lucky then a mutha fucka," Booker shook his head, smiling, thinking of past memories. "But yea, man. Shit got real before my last speech and the next thing I know, I'm simp'n on the runway."

"Y'all was over there looking like soulmates." Manny joked in a quiet room. Only to look over, seeing Booker stare off smiling, licking his bottom lip in middle of a daydream.

"Did you…?" Manny asked without asking.

Booker's bubble burst and he had to think quick. He chuckled, asking, "When? Shit, where? That's the better question." Booker asked.

"Right. You did say it just popped off yesterday and we stayed on the move. Now she's on her way back to the East Coast and it didn't get too serious. That's like a summer crush at camp back in the day. As soon as you tell her you like her, it's time to go home. That should make things a little easier."

Booker waited before speaking then said, "I miss her, dawg. I can't een lie to you. Chicks like her make ya slow down."

Ring, Ring, Ring.

Booker reached in his pocket for his phone and said, "Ohhh shit!" Showing Manny, Lina's name on the screen.

"Booker Garvey III." Manny shook his head, smirking. "You a wild boy, dawg."

Preamble

POTUS 2028 PREVIEW:
(POTUS 2028 begins at the end of POTUS 2024)

"Mannn, I don't try to be." Booker admitted. "What do I do?" He asked as his phone kept ringing.

"Answer, Playboy." Manny laughed, waiting for the drama to unfold.

"Hello?" Booker answered.

"You are alive—," Lina said. Then she hung up on him.

"Hello?" He went once and a second time. "Hello?" Looking at Manny, he said, "She just hung up."

"Did she say anything?" Manny asked.

"Yeah. She said, *You are alive* and hung up."

Manny laughed before saying, "She's sick of yo shit, bro."

"I see." Booker hung his head, saying, "Damn."

"You gon call her back?" Manny asked.

"After you leave. She prolly gon cut into me." Booker admitted.

"Or cut… yo ass off. You wild'n, Book." Manny laughed. "I'm glad I got out the game. I don't wanna be a playa no mo." Manny shook his head.

"Takes too much time and concentration."

"Concentration?"

"Yeah, man. You see how often I post shit in the wrong chat."

"Yeah, you woulda *been* caught up. That's because y'all be lying to these women. I'd tell them the truth and let them decide."

"Then call her back."

"Shiiit. Just because you tell them the truth doesn't make it easy." He rejected by countering, "It just makes it easi*er*."

"I hear you." Manny laughed before weighing Booker's options. "Lina's down as fuck. I think she'd ride or die for yo ass, literally." Manny was nodding as he spoke.

"Monica is prolly top five baddest chicks I've ever seen in real life and she cool as fuck."

"Dawg," Booker agreed. "Ol fine… cool ass."

Manny chuckled. "What's the other one's name? Austria? Somalia?"

"Kenya, man." Booker chuckled, correcting him. "Kenya."

"I knew it was a country." Manny laughed, asking, "What about her? What she bring to the table?"

"Culture. She's cultured than a muh fucka. She got that natural beauty. She don't wear makeup. But her skin glows, bruh. You'd bet she did."

"That smooth ass, cocoa butter skin, huh?"

"Dawg. A lil chocolate drop, too. I'd eat her lil ass up, bro." Booker shook his head, showing Manny her pictures.

Manny chuckled. "Yeah, that's yo type, fasho. She rock'n a gele. African garb n'shit."

"Yeah, man. She's one hundred percent Kenyan. Her moms ran for Miss World Kenya in the 80s before she got prego. They moved here when she was little."

"Damn, bro. You got a problem most muh fuckas dream about. Three baddies on ya team."

"It ain't as easy as it looks, bruh. It might be fun… but it ain't easy." Booker slouched in his seat. "I want em all." Hesitating, he said, "I want my cake and eat it too. The fuck I'm supposed to do!?" His words were intense.

"Just like a n—"

Before Manny could finish his sentence, Booker's phone vibrated in his hand. "Speak of the angel," Manny said. Then he gave Booker his phone back.

"Kenya, Kenya, Kenya." Booker shook his head, smiling. Opening the text thread, he read it aloud.

Kenya, Kenya, Kenya

Today 1:45 PM

> I just wanted to tell you how proud I am of you. You've come a long way since you were venting to your megaphone. Now, you're a real Politician!

> I hope you keep running. You're the man this country needs.
>
> I can't wait to get to know you better. I know you're busy, tired, or both but I just wanted you to know that you are appreciated. I'm not talking about by me. We haven't known each other that long yet. Like you said in your speech, you sidetracked your youth for students you don't know and families you never met. Now, you're doing the same thing as a Politician. You are AMAZING! Reply or call when you can! 😘😘😘

Looking at Manny, he said, "How the fuck I'm supposed to choose between a ryda, Mother Nature, and a super baddie? That's three different wants, needs, and desires, dawg. They bring three completely different things to the table."

"Who brings the most you *need* from a woman?" Manny asked. "And in what order are those needs. Major and minor needs don't balance the scale." Manny used his hands as scales.

"Real spill." They chuckled.

"I don't need to know, G. But that answer, answers your question."

As the day moved on to the next, things were almost back to normal. The Party was back in the DMV area, Manny was in Detroit, and Booker was officially back to his old ways.

Ring, ring, ring.

The phone continued to ring without an answer. Booker was receiving what he dished out in full. A text message was his next move.

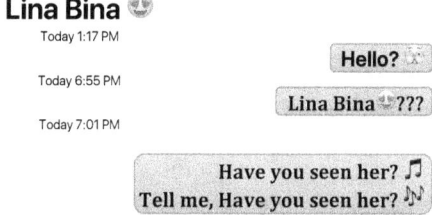

Booker waited a while before making another unsuccessful contact attempt. Afterwards, he sat in peace thinking about his next move.

XV: I Think I Love You Too

Over the last two months, Booker made a smooth transition back to his normal day to day routines. Some were a bit easier to adjust to than others.
Ring, ring, ring!
"Hello?" Booker answered, smiling.
"Hi, Baby!?" Monica greeted him full of energy.
"Wassup, Sweetie. How you?" He replied.
"Gooood. What are you doing for Dr. King's Day?"
"Today? Or the twentieth?"
"It is his birthday today, huh?" She acknowledged. "Happy birthday, Dr. King." She wished from the other side.
"Happy birthday, Dr. King!" Booker echoed. "But that's a good question. I'm still on sabbatical. My first day back is after spring break.
"I'm going to finish the year. Retire. Do this author thing until the POTUS 2024 book run slows down. So probably around the end of the year." He thought.
"Then I'm back on the campaign trail with Mrs. Jarreau!" Booker joked. "Long story short, not a damn shit!"
"You are so silly." Monica laughed.
"She told my black ass *Mrs.*, three times!" He shouted with animation. "Mrs. Jarreau, Mrs. J. Manny said you told him Mrs. Monica."
Their laughter paused the conversation. "How many muh fuckas you got running around here calling you Mrs. J?" Booker asked to more laughter. "The only Mrs. J I know is Mrs. Julene!"
Monica laughed so hard; she made a loud shrieking noise. "What the fuck was that?" His question made her do it again.
With their conversation returning to the purpose of the call, Monica began speaking. "I miss laughing with your funny self. I was wonderinn…"

Dragging the word gave Booker time to think. *Kzoo is wayyy too small to take her out here. Sis and Cuz were trying to do a game night. I can have her fly into the city and meet her at DTW.*

An entire play ran through Booker's mind while she finished the word. "nnnnng…"

POTUS 2028:
Coming Soon

Critical Thinking Topic Starters: 1-11

(Submit your answers to: The Realist Critical Thinking Party's Headquarters.)

1. Booker has a few full circle moments, which did you notice? What did you think of them?

2. Describe Booker's development over the year 2024 and into 2025. What stood out most to you? Why?

3. Would you ever consider politics? Why? Why not?

4. Booker exudes confidence. But a couple times throughout the book, he faces adversity within himself. What do you think propelled him through those times? What would you do to get through those kinds of moments?

5. What would you tell Booker after his campaign run?

6. What were your favorite moments from Booker's presidential campaign? What didn't you like? What would you change?

7. What did you think about POTUS 2024?

8. What are your thoughts on the POTUS 2028 Preview?

9. What are you most excited for about POTUS 2028? When do you want it to be released?

10. What initiatives would you like to see the Realist Critical Thinking Party address during their 2028 Race for the White House?

11. Send a message to someone from The Party: Booker, Julene, Lenice, Isaac, Jasmine, Monica, Claudine, Manny, Norman, or the entire Realist Critical Thinking Party.

Realist Critical Thinking Party:

Booking/Inquires

POTUS 2024: BALANCE THE SCALE

BLACK LASSO

B. GARVEY III

LADY ATLANTIS

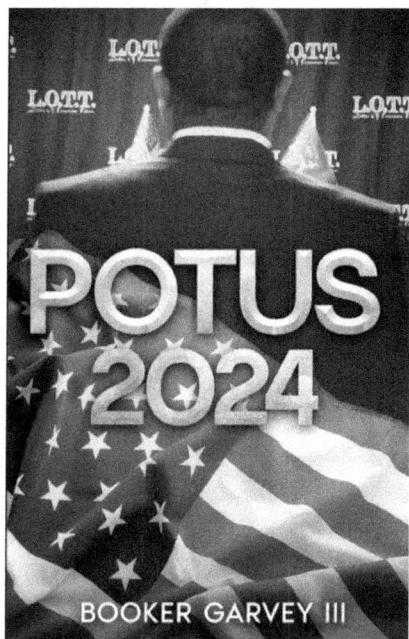

ABOUT THE AUTHOR

Booker Garvey III is an American author from Highland Park, Michigan. He has roots in other cities like the Brightmoor neighborhood in Detroit, Kalamazoo, and Ypsilanti, through his career as a student and educator. Garvey started writing with Leaders of Tomorrow, Today… in 2014 as an Intern.

After learning the ropes, Garvey fast tracked his Writing career as an independent author. He ventured off to write blogs, short stories, another novel, and he's also penned a children's book.

POTUS 2024 is Garvey's first publication with Leaders of Tomorrow, Today. After signing a one project deal, Garvey is currently in contract negotiations for his follow up project, *POTUS 2028*.

B. GARVEY III

Michigan International University (2015)

Wake Up Little Lion (2016)

Nobody Cares (2019)   Bad Move (2020)   Prize Fighter (2022)

www.LOTT.com/shop

10 YEARS OF EXCELLENCE

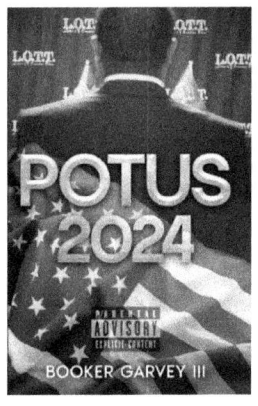
POTUS 2024 (2025)

www.ingramcontent.com/pod-product-compliance
Lightning Source LLC
LaVergne TN
LVHW051553070426
835507LV00021B/2554